CRABTREE GROUNDBREAKER BIOGRAPHIES

Muhammad Ali

THE GREATEST

By Susan Brophy Down

Crabtree Publishing Company
www.crabtreebooks.com

Crabtree Publishing Company
www.crabtreebooks.com

Author: Susan Brophy Down
Publishing plan research and development:
  Sean Charlebois, Reagan Miller
  Crabtree Publishing Company
Project coordinator: Mark Sachner,
  Water Buffalo Books
Editors: Mark Sachner, Lynn Peppas
Proofreader: Wendy Scavuzzo
Indexer: Gini Holland
Editorial director: Kathy Middleton
Photo researcher: Ruth Owen
Designer: Alix Wood
Production coordinator: Margaret Amy Salter
Production: Kim Richardson
Prepress technician: Margaret Amy Salter
Print coordinator: Katherine Berti

Written, developed, and produced by
Water Buffalo Books

Photographs and reproductions:
Corbis: David James: p. 1; Bettmann: pp. 8, 10,
  37 (right), 51, 66, 77, 80; dpa: p. 39 (left); Donald L.
  Robinson: p. 60; Lynn Goldsmith: p. 83; Andy
  Clarik: p. 93
Dreamstime: cover (background).
Getty Images: Jerry Cooke: p. 17; Neil Leifer: p. 19
  (left); Gamma-Keystone: p. 27. Public domain:
  cover (inset); pp. 4 (inset), 12 (all), 14, 21, 22, 24, 25,
  31 (left), 32, 41, 54 (right), 57, 68, 74, 78, 91, 103 (left)
Shutterstock: Featureflash: pp. 4, 81, 85 (bottom), 99;
  Neftali: pp. 5, 6, 19 (right), 35, 36, 53, 54 (left), 58, 59,
  61, 71, 72, 73, 75, 87, 89; Alt Eduard: pp. 9, 15, 16, 20,
  21, 64, 65, 84, 90, 92, 94, 95, 100, 101, 102, 103 (right);
  Jorg Hackemann: pp. 28, 29, 30, 31 (right), 38, 39
  (right), 44, 45; Stocklight: p. 85 (top).
Superstock: pp. 26, 49
Wikipedia Creative Commons: Marsyas: p. 7;
  Angelo and Giorgio Bonomo: p. 37 (left); Mark
  Pellegrini: p. 97.

Publisher's note:
All quotations in this book come from original sources
and contain the spelling and grammatical inconsistencies
of the original text. Some of the quotations may also
contain terms that are no longer in use and may be
considered inappropriate or offensive. The use of such
terms is for the sake of preserving the historical and
literary accuracy of the sources and should not be seen
as encouraging or endorsing the use of such terms today.

Cover: Heavyweight champ Muhammad Ali lands a
left against challenger Leon Spinks in their fight on
February 15, 1978. Spinks defeated Ali in a 15-round
decision, becoming the only boxer ever to take the
title from Ali. In a rematch in September that same
year, Ali won the crown back for an unprecedented
third time.

Library and Archives Canada Cataloguing in Publication

Down, Susan Brophy
    Muhammad Ali : the greatest / Susan Brophy Down.

(Crabtree groundbreaker biographies)
Includes index.
Issued also in electronic formats.
ISBN 978-0-7787-1034-9 (bound).--ISBN 978-0-7787-1043-1 (pbk.)

    1. Ali, Muhammad, 1942- --Juvenile literature. 2. Boxers
(Sports)--United States--Biography--Juvenile literature. I. Title.
II. Series: Crabtree groundbreaker biographies

GV1132.A44D69 2013   j796.83092   C2012-908253-8

Library of Congress Cataloging-in-Publication Data

Down, Susan Brophy.
    Muhammad Ali : the greatest / Susan Brophy Down.
        pages cm. -- (Crabtree groundbreaker biographies)
    Includes index.
    ISBN 978-0-7787-1034-9 (reinforced library binding) -- ISBN 978-
0-7787-1043-1 (pbk.) -- ISBN 978-1-4271-9246-2 (electronic (pdf))
-- ISBN 978-1-4271-9170-0 (electronic (html))
    1. Ali, Muhammad, 1942---Juvenile literature. 2. African American
boxers--Biography--Juvenile literature. 3. Boxers (Sports)--United
States--Biography--Juvenile literature. I. Title.
    GV1132.A4D69 2013
    796.83092--dc23
    [B]
                                        2012048490

Crabtree Publishing Company

www.crabtreebooks.com   1-800-387-7650   Printed in Canada/012013/MA20121217

Published
in Canada
Crabtree Publishing
616 Welland Ave.
St. Catharines, Ontario
L2M 5V6

Published in
the United States
Crabtree Publishing
PMB 59051
350 Fifth Ave., 59th Floor
New York, NY 10118

Published in the
United Kingdom
Crabtree Publishing
Maritime House
Basin Road North, Hove
BN41 1WR

Published
in Australia
Crabtree Publishing
3 Charles Street
Coburg North
VIC, 3058

Contents

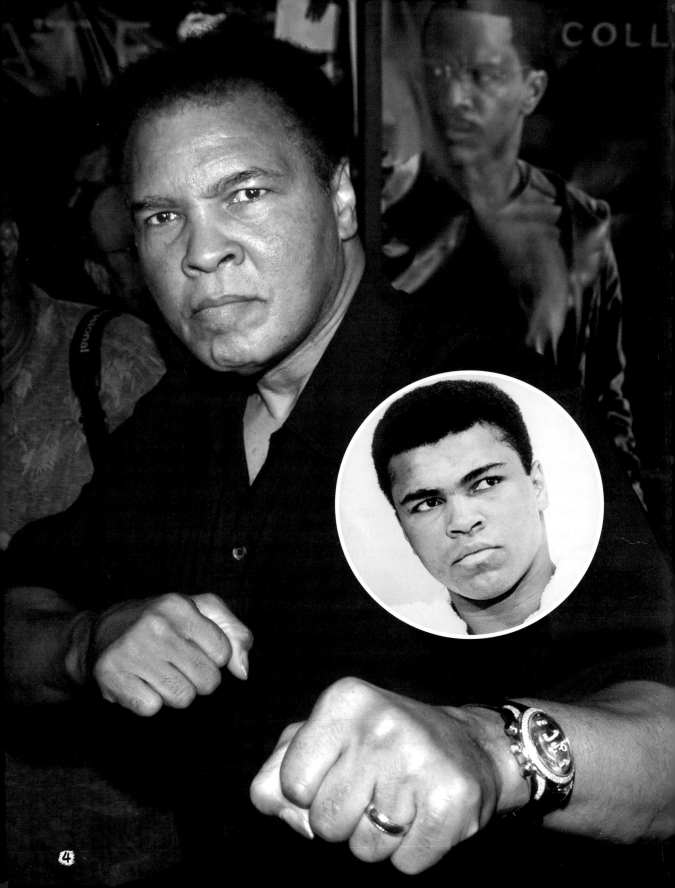

Chapter 1
Facing Fear on the Road to Gold

Boxing was a passion for young teenager Cassius Clay. But, even with his new skills, he was still afraid of the local bully. Corky Baker was older than Clay and had a reputation at their high school as a mean and strong fighter who earned money by betting people how high he could lift the end of a car. He intimidated kids in his Louisville, Kentucky, neighborhood by demanding money as a toll if they wanted to walk past him.

Beating the Bully

Clay knew that he had to confront this bully or he would never have complete confidence in his abilities. He didn't want to have a fistfight in the street without any rules or a referee, however, so he started telling people that he could beat Baker in the boxing ring. This made Baker furious. But he was reluctant to try boxing, calling it a sport for sissies. Baker's

Above: A postage stamp from Austria honors Muhammad Ali.

Opposite: Muhammad Ali mugs for the camera at the Los Angeles world premier of the 2004 crime thriller Collateral. *Despite the passage of time since his boxing career and failing health, Ali continues to be the object of attention and admiration wherever he goes. Inset: Muhammad Ali in 1967, the year he was stripped of his heavyweight boxing title for refusing induction into the U.S. Army.*

classmates pointed out that if he didn't want to box, then that meant Baker must be scared. Baker agreed to meet Clay.

The plan was to fight three rounds for the right to be called King of the Street. Baker rushed at Clay, aiming strong punches at his body. Clay was fast enough to evade Baker's fists, and he was able to land enough punches to give Baker a black eye and bloody nose. "Before the second round was over, [Baker] said, 'This ain't fair' and ran out of the ring and left the gym," recalled Clay. "I had won the respect of my peers." The neighborhood kids were delighted because, after that, Baker didn't pick on anyone anymore. Most importantly, Clay had overcome his fear of the bully.

A Lesson for Life

Only a few years later, as a young adult, Cassius Clay (later known as Muhammad Ali) faced even more formidable foes in his personal and professional life. He fought the government to stay true to his beliefs. He also fought the boxing world for taking away his opportunity to box as a professional. After all his battles inside and outside the ring, he became a hugely popular figure who was proud of his religion and his African-American heritage.

He supported human rights and contributed to many projects that improved people's lives. His early encounter in the playground and boxing ring gave him the self-confidence he needed to become a role model. People all over the world admired his strength and sense of charity.

A BRIEF HISTORY OF BOXING

The sport of boxing has been a popular contest of strength, endurance, and skill for centuries. It was included in the original Olympic Games in Ancient Greece over 2,000 years ago.

Early fighters wrapped their fists with strips of leather that were tied around their arms. Later, as the sport grew in popularity, bare-knuckle prizefighting was replaced by fighting with padded gloves, especially in Britain and North America. A boxing match takes place in a ring, which is on a platform surrounded by ropes. Each round is two to three minutes long, followed by a one-minute rest period. Title fights were once 15 rounds, but boxing officials shortened this to 12 rounds in the 1980s. The boxers compete in different weight classes from flyweight to heavyweight.

In this ancient Greek wall art, two young boys are shown boxing.

688 B.C. Boxing is included in the Olympic Games in Ancient Greece.

1600s Fistfighting becomes a popular spectator sport in Britain.

1743 Jack Broughton, the first British heavyweight champ, introduces a set of seven rules to standardize boxing. He also invents the first boxing gloves, used only for practice.

1838 The London Prize Ring rules are added to Broughton's rules to make the sport safer.

1867 The Marquess of Queensbury rules are adopted to improve fair play and sportsmanship. Three-minute rounds are introduced.

1882 Gloved boxing is introduced.

1913 Mouthguards are first used in the ring.

2012 Women's boxing makes its first appearance at the Olympics, at the London Games.

One Last Fear to Overcome

Clay had to face another fear before he began the road to becoming a champ in the boxing ring. When he attended the trials for the 1960 U.S. Olympic team, he flew on a plane for the first time from Kentucky to California. The turbulent ride really frightened him, and he didn't want to board a plane ever again. When Clay earned a spot on the boxing team, he realized that meant flying again if he was going to get to Rome, where the Olympic Games were held that year. He tried to talk his trainers into letting him go professional and skipping the Olympics.

Members of the 1960 U.S. Olympic boxing team gather for a group photo. Cassius Clay, then 18 years old, is at the far right.

Tall and muscular, Clay didn't look like he was afraid of anything. He loved to talk, boasting that he was going to be the greatest boxer ever. During his teenage years as an amateur, Clay had boxed more than 100 times, with only a few losses. Climbing into a ring to face an opponent and his powerful punches didn't intimidate him. But flying was different. His coach told him that the only way to make it to the Olympic Games on time was to fly with the rest of the U.S. team. So Clay bought a parachute at an army-navy surplus store and insisted on wearing it during the flight. There was a lot of turbulence during the hours in the air, and Clay was reportedly praying for his safety.

Clay's Unique Style

Once in Rome, Clay and the rest of the boxing team got down to training seriously. Clay was already an award-winning boxer with six Golden Gloves wins in Kentucky. He also had won four national titles. Two of those were Golden Gloves and two were Amateur Athletic Union (AAU) titles. During his amateur years, he had lost only a handful of fights.

THE GOLDEN GLOVES

A Chicago sportswriter suggested the idea of a competition for non-professional fighters and, since 1928, these U.S. regional contests have been known as the Golden Gloves. The competition is limited to amateur boxers over 16, and the winners from the regional contests go on to compete in the national finals. Former amateur champions who became renowned professionals include Joe Louis, Sonny Liston, and Cassius Clay.

Clay had developed his own unusual style of boxing. Instead of using the classic stance—holding his hands up higher to protect his face—he held his fists lower at his waist and relied on his quick reflexes to evade the punches aimed at him. He also pranced and danced in the ring, a style that was seen in the lighter weight classes but unheard of in the heavyweight division. Heavier fighters generally stood toe-to-toe and slugged one another. The combination of fast feet and hands was known as a "stick and move" approach. He quickly landed a flurry of jabs, then slid away out of reach before his opponent had a chance to react.

His height and long arms gave him the ability to punch from a distance that some other boxers couldn't reach. He could also move his head out of the way of a bruising punch so quickly that it made his opponents look clumsy and awkward as they swung at the air.

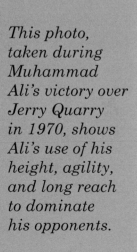

This photo, taken during Muhammad Ali's victory over Jerry Quarry in 1970, shows Ali's use of his height, agility, and long reach to dominate his opponents.

Winning at Boxing

A boxing bout can be won in several different ways—by a knockout, technical knockout, or decision. A knockout occurs by knocking the opponent to the floor. If he stays there for 10 seconds, the referee calls the other boxer the winner of the fight by a knockout. A technical knockout (TKO) happens when a bout is stopped by a referee or trainer or the boxer himself because the fighter is too injured to continue. Finally, a fighter can win by decision. In that case, three judges score each fighter based on the number of successful punches and decide the winner. A split decision means one of the judges disagreed with the other two. If a boxing match lasts for the allotted 12 rounds, the fighters are said to have "gone the distance." When Clay was starting his career, boxing matches could last for 15 rounds. Olympic boxing matches are only 3 rounds.

Fighting for Gold in Rome

In his first match, Clay won in the second round against a fighter from Belgium. His next fight was against a fighter from the Soviet Union who was the gold medalist from the last Olympic Games. Clay won a unanimous decision and moved on to the semi-finals against an Australian, again receiving a 5-0 decision from the judges.

In the finals, Clay had to fight a Polish boxer, Zbigniew Pietrzykowski, a veteran who had earned a bronze medal at the 1956 Olympics four years before. His opponent was very skilled and 10 years older than Clay. He was also left handed, a factor that can confuse a fighter who

LEGENDS OF THE RING

Jack Johnson, the son of former slaves, was the first African-American world heavyweight champion when he won in 1908. Johnson dropped out of school and became a dockworker. He was a cautious, clever fighter nicknamed the "Galveston Giant." His fight against a white man named James Jeffries in 1910 became a competition between the races. His victory caused African Americans all over the United States to celebrate in the streets. He held his title until 1915. He liked to spend money on expensive cars and jewelry. He was married three times to white women, which shocked people at the time. He boxed until 1946 when, at age 60, he was killed in a car accident.

Jack Johnson

Jack Dempsey was the world heavyweight champion from 1919 to 1926. His fights were also a financial success—he was the first boxer to generate $1 million in ticket sales at the gate. Born in Colorado, Dempsey was a Mormon who was part Irish and part Cherokee. While defending his title, he was once knocked through the ropes and onto a reporter's typewriter. After losing his title to Gene Tunney in 1926, he told his wife, "Honey, I forgot to duck." In retirement, he appeared in movies and opened a restaurant in New York. He joined the U.S. Coast Guard reserve to serve in World War II. He fought 83 times as a pro and lost only 6 times.

Jack Dempsey

Joe Louis, nicknamed the "Brown Bomber," learned to fight as a boy in Detroit. After he won the light heavyweight Detroit Golden Gloves championship, he turned professional and became one of the most beloved fighters in the nation. In the eyes of many of his fans, his wins during the decade before World War II represented an upholding of U.S. national honor. He lost his first fight against German heavyweight champ Max Schmeling in 1936, then defeated him in the rematch in 1938. This was a win that many saw as a defeat for Nazi leader Adolf Hitler and his belief in racial superiority. Louis was heavyweight champ for 11 years, from 1937 to 1948. He is known as one of the greatest heavyweight champions ever. He also served in the U.S. Army during World War II.

Joe Louis

is used to opponents who are right handed. During the first round, Clay was pounded by the older opponent. In the second round, he started to get his rhythm back and landed a few punches. Clay knew, however, that if he was to add more points to his score and win the match in the third and final round, he needed to deliver as many punches as he could. Clay peppered the Polish boxer with punches and received another 5-0 unanimous decision from the judges—and the gold medal. He was part of a talented U.S. boxing squad that year. Two other members of the team also earned gold for the U.S. in their weight classes.

The Golden Boy

Thanks to his victory, Clay's prediction that he would win no longer sounded like a wild claim from a young hopeful. Now it had come true. He had trained hard for his medal, and he was so proud of his achievement that he wore it everywhere for two days, even sleeping with his gold medal around his neck.

Cassius Clay was also a performer outside the ring. With his exuberant personality and talkative nature, he charmed the other athletes, who called him the mayor of the athletes' Olympic Village. When he wasn't training, he walked around the Village, meeting people from every country and exchanging national pins with them as souvenirs. One sour note came when a reporter from the Soviet Union asked him why, as a gold medalist, he still wouldn't be admitted to some hotels and restaurants back home because of his race. Clay answered in a patriotic style. "To me, the USA is still the best

"We'd walk around and he'd go up to people and shake hands with them, but he had his mind on training. He worked for that gold medal. He trained very, very hard."

Wilbert "Skeeter" McClure, Cassius Clay's Olympic roommate

1960 Rome Olympics

Athletes from 83 countries participated when Italy hosted the 1960 Olympic Games in Rome, the first summer Olympics to be broadcast on television in North America. The Rome Olympics are remembered not only for launching the career of Cassius Clay, but also for the achievements by black Africans. Clement Quartey from Ghana was the first black African to win an Olympic medal when he won silver in light welterweight boxing. Then marathon runner Abebe Bikila of Ethiopia ran and won the grueling race barefoot to become the first-ever black African to win a gold medal.

African Americans were also stars. Cassius Clay won the gold medal in light heavyweight boxing, and sprinter Wilma Rudolph won an amazing three gold medals on the track, even though she was severely disabled by polio as a child and wore a brace on her leg for several years.

The 1960 Games are also noted as the last time the repressive apartheid regime of South Africa was permitted to attend. Apartheid meant that even though the majority of the country's population was black, the rights of black Africans were limited and the government was run by members of the white minority. The country was allowed to return to the Olympics many years later, in 1992, when it began to reform its policies and prepared to hold multi-racial democratic elections.

U.S. sprinter Wilma Rudolph, considered the fastest woman in the world in the 1960s, is shown crossing the finish line in 1961, the year following her triumphant appearance at the 1960 Summer Olympics in Rome.

country in the world, including yours," he said, adding that his country had experts who were working on the issue of how to stop prejudice against black people.

Despite this and other distractions, it was difficult to tarnish Clay's medal achievement. He wrote a poem—the first of many to come in his career—to further enhance his reputation as a boxer and an entertainer:

"To make America the greatest is my goal.
So I beat the Russian and I beat the Pole
And for the USA won the medal of gold.
Italians said 'You're greater than the
Cassius of Old.
We like your name, we like your game
So make Rome your home if you will.'
I said I appreciate your kind hospitality
But the USA is my country still
Cause they are waiting to welcome
me in Louisville."

"I didn't take that medal off for 48 hours. I even wore it to bed. I didn't sleep too good because I had to sleep on my back so that the medal wouldn't cut me. But I didn't care, I was Olympic champion."

Cassius Clay

Back home again, Clay wore his Olympic blazer and gold medal with pride. Still, he was surprised that so many people who had seen him on TV recognized him. Clay rode in a parade in his honor through the streets of Louisville, and the city's mayor told him the gold medal was Clay's key to the city.

Gold Medal Mystery, Golden Career Ahead

One mystery is what happened to the gold medal that never left Clay's side. Probably the best-known story, based on Muhammad Ali's 1975 autobiography, is that he threw it away after returning home and witnessing firsthand that nothing had changed regarding the treatment of African Americans. He has also claimed that he just lost it. Whether he lost it or threw it away intentionally is still unclear.

Outside the boxing ring, he would receive honors and accolades well beyond anything he could have imagined as a little boy from Kentucky.

Either way, Clay's golden future was just beginning, and the medal would be only the first in a series of awards and achievements in his sparkling career. In 1996, when he lit the Olympic flame during the Atlanta Olympic Games, he was given a replacement medal. In the 26 years between those two sporting events, as Muhammad Ali, he would become one of the most recognizable people in the world—not just for his boxing achievements, but also for his humanitarian deeds and his firm stance against war. Outside the boxing ring, he would receive honors and accolades well beyond anything he could have imagined as a little boy from Kentucky.

U.S. boxing gold medal winners at the 1960 Rome Olympics pose for a group portrait: From left to right: Wilbert McClure (light middleweight), Cassius Clay (light heavyweight), and Eddie Crook Jr. (middleweight).

Chapter 2
Early Hooks and Jabs

Muhammad Ali was born as Cassius Marcellus Clay Jr. on January 17, 1942, in Louisville, the largest city in Kentucky. The baby was named after his father, Cassius Sr., an artist who painted murals and signs. His mother, Odessa, worked as a domestic servant for white families in town. They weren't rich, but compared to the impoverished childhoods of some of the boxers Clay would meet later in his career, they were well off. They owned their home, and Odessa brought up Cassius and his brother Rudy in the Southern Baptist Church.

Muhammad Ali kisses his mother, Odessa Clay, while his father, Cassius Clay Sr., playfully tugs on his son's arm as Ali trains for his 1974 fight with George Foreman in Africa.

A Segregated World

Clay's heritage was mixed. His great-grandfather was from Ireland, but most of his ancestors were brought to the United States as slaves before the Civil War (1861–1865). Clay's name sounded regal—Cassius was a senator in Ancient Rome. Another Cassius Marcellus Clay was a white Kentucky landowner who fought to end slavery 100 years before. Clay later rejected his name because it was his "slave" name. Africans were forced to take new last names when the arrived in the United States. Often they were given the last names, or surnames, of their masters.

Clay grew up in a black neighborhood in Louisville at a time of racial segregation in the South. Segregation meant that black people and white people were separated according to local laws At the time, there were many places in the city where Clay and other African Americans were forbidden to go. On a bus, they had to sit at the back, and many restaurants, hotels, and stores were "white only," which meant they would not serve African-American customers. Clay thought this was wrong.

Even after the Civil War and the freeing of the slaves, in the eyes of many white people, African Americans were still considered inferior and separated from white society. In addition to official racial segregation, white terrorist organizations such as the Ku Klux Klan used violence to intimidate black people and enforce their agenda of hate. Wearing white hoods to disguise themselves, they burned churches and schools and tortured and murdered African Americans, Jews, and members of other ethnic

SLAVE NAMES

Before the Civil War, slavery was still practiced in the United States, especially in the South. The slaves were brought over from African countries and given new last names. Sometimes these surnames related to the slave's work (for example, "Cotton"), and sometimes they were given their master's last name. After slavery was abolished, these African Americans either kept their slave masters' names or changed their names to that of a president, such as Washington or Jackson, or simply to Freeman.

In the 20th century, some African Americans changed their names to Arabic ones, reflecting their new Muslim religious beliefs. For example, basketball star Ferdinand Lewis Alcindor changed his name to Kareem Abdul-Jabbar in the early 1970s. When Cassius Clay joined the Nation of Islam, he called himself Cassius X because he believed Clay was his slave name, and he later took the new name Muhammad Ali.

In more recent times, inspired by African languages such as Zulu or Swahili, many parents have chosen distinctive African-American first names for their children.

Lew Alcindor, shown here playing for UCLA in 1967, converted to Islam in 1968 and took the name that most people know him by today— Kareem Abdul-Jabbar.

groups. News stories and graphic photographs of these events, such as the murder of 14-year-old Emmett Till—an African-American boy accused of flirting with a white woman in Mississippi—influenced Clay deeply, since he was about the same age at the time.

Clay wasn't an exceptional student. In fact, his high school teachers would later make sure he graduated despite his poor grades, because

Jim Crow Laws

From 1876 until 1965, many state and local laws segregated white and African-American citizens in the South so that they lived very separate lives. Under these laws, known as Jim Crow laws, African Americans weren't allowed to attend the same schools or even drink from the same water fountains as white people. Movie theaters and restaurants were either completely segregated as to race or had separate seating areas within the same buildings. For example, buses had a section in the back for "colored" people. In 1954, the U.S. Supreme Court ruled that segregation was illegal in education. The rest of the local laws were abolished under the Civil Rights Act of 1964 and the Voting Rights Act of 1965.

An African-American boy stands at a "colored" drinking fountain on a courthouse lawn in North Carolina, 1938.

EMMETT TILL

The murder of Emmett Till outraged Americans and was considered a central event in the push for African-American rights and justice. Till was a 14-year-old Chicago boy visiting relatives in Money, Mississippi, during his summer vacation in 1955. His mother had warned him about the South's more conservative attitudes and urged him to be careful, but he boasted to local kids that he had a white girlfriend back home. On a dare, he walked into a local grocery store and said something sassy to the young white cashier who was the owner's wife. A few nights later, two men pulled Till out of bed and took him to a barn where they beat, tortured, and shot him before throwing his body into the river with a heavy fan wrapped around his neck.

After the body was discovered, the store owner and his half-brother were arrested and charged with murder. The jury of 12 white men acquitted the pair after just over an hour of deliberation.

A few months later, however, the accused men confessed to a journalist that they had murdered Till. By then, they were protected by double jeopardy laws that prevent a person from standing trial twice for the same crime. Till's mother insisted on a glass-topped coffin so her son's injuries could be visible, and extensive media coverage showed pictures of the body. Decades later, in 2004, the U.S. Department of Justice reopened the case but did not charge any other suspects. In 2007, Tallahatchie County, Mississippi, issued an official apology to the Till family for the miscarriage of justice.

they could see his boxing talent would take him a long way. He had other gifts besides academics. He loved to talk. His father said he often came home from work and saw his son enthusiastically telling stories to a group of boys on the porch.

Changing Society

The world was changing for African Americans while Clay was growing up. Just before he was born in 1942, the United States had entered World War II. Although the U.S. military was still mostly segregated along racial lines, many politicians and ordinary citizens began arguing against segregated military units, particularly in light of the heroic service of many African-American soldiers, sailors, and airmen during the war. In the years following the war, the military began to take on the character that everyone accepts as the norm today—soldiers of all races and ethnic backgrounds serving side by side.

Members of the Tuskegee Airmen, the first squadron of African-American pilots trained in the U.S. military, are shown during a briefing session in 1945. The Tuskegee Airmen served with distinction during World War II, inspiring many Americans and helping advance the desegregation of U.S. fighting units after the war. The pilots were also the subject of a 1995 HBO movie and a 2012 feature film, Red Tails.

Racial barriers were being broken in sports, too. In 1947, Jackie Robinson became the first black major league baseball player when he joined the Brooklyn Dodgers. In basketball today, about 80 percent of pro players are African American. It's hard to believe that people of all races were not allowed to play in the National Basketball Association until 1950.

Discovering His Destiny

The story of Cassius Clay's discovery of the sport of boxing has been told often. His interest in boxing began when he was 12 years old after a chance meeting with a man who would be one of the most important influences in Clay's early career. Clay was attending a local event at the old Columbia Auditorium with his friends, hoping to enjoy some of the free food samples the merchants were handing out. During the day, he discovered that his prized bicycle had

Jackie Robinson, shown here in 1954, was a pioneer in breaking the so-called color barrier in baseball and other big-league sports. When Robinson was signed to play for the Brooklyn Dodgers, he became the first—and, at that time, the only—African-American player to don a major league baseball uniform.

been stolen. Very angry, he reported the theft to a local policeman named Joe Martin. When Clay said he wanted to beat up the thieves if they were ever caught, Martin didn't want him to get into trouble. In his spare time, Martin just happened to be a boxing coach at the Columbia Gym, and he produced a TV program called *Tomorrow's Champions* highlighting local amateur boxers. Martin was always happy to have a new student join the boxing team. He suggested that the boy learn how to fight before pursuing the bicycle thieves.

Even in his earliest days as a fighter, Muhammad Ali (then Cassius Clay), was quick to declare himself "the greatest."

Chasing the Dream

Pretty soon, Clay was a regular at the gym. He had thought about football, but he wanted to play a sport in which he would stand out and be recognized rather than participate in a team event. Boxing was perfect for the slender, agile boy who liked to dance around in the ring. Just weeks after he started boxing, Clay won his first fight.

His matches attracted an audience right from the start because of the way he boasted about his talent before the event. "People would go out of their way to come and see me, hoping I would get beat," he said. Even then he said "I am the greatest"—a phrase that he repeated often in his professional years.

Martin saw Clay's natural abilities and was able to encourage and help the boy develop into a fighter of Olympic caliber. Clay also worked with boxing trainer Fred Stoner, who would later be the first African American on the Kentucky Boxing Commission.

Clay worked hard at his training, not only practicing and exercising whenever he could, but also paying attention to his diet. He ran and skipped rope to improve his already fast reflexes. For breakfast, he drank a big glass of milk with two raw eggs mixed in. He didn't smoke or drink alcohol. He was very dedicated to improving himself, something his coach noticed right away.

Thrilled by this early success, Clay devoted himself to learning what some writers called

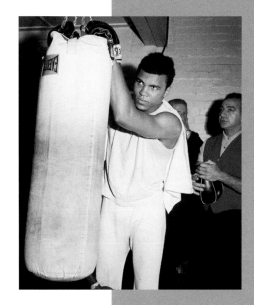

Cassius Clay in training during the 1960s

"He stood out because he had more determination than most boys. He was a kid willing to make the sacrifices necessary to achieve something worthwhile in sports. It was almost impossible to discourage him. He was easily the hardest worker of any kid I ever taught."

Joe Martin, coach

"the sweet science of boxing." He asked teenage friends to hold their hands up so he could punch at them. His reflexes had always been fast, but he was always trying to find ways to improve his skills. His brother Rudy once talked about what it was like to work with Cassius on one of his unorthodox training methods:

> *"All the time, he used to ask me to throw rocks at him. I thought he was crazy, but he'd dodge every one. No matter how many I threw, I could never hit him."*

Clay paid attention to general fitness as well as boxing technique. Instead of riding the school bus in the morning, he raced it to school, passing it every time the driver stopped to pick up another student. He did his early morning runs in heavy boots to make him stronger.

Astonishing Amateur

In 1958, at the age of 16, Clay found that his devoted training schedule had begun to pay off. He won the amateur-championship Golden Gloves in his hometown of Louisville.

The following year, he won the national light-heavyweight Golden Gloves title as well as the AAU title. Even though he had plenty of muscle on his tall frame, he was still a slim young boy. In 1960, however, he moved up a weight class to the heavyweight division so he wouldn't have to fight his younger brother Rudy, who was also a promising boxer. He beat defending champion Jimmy Jones in the Chicago finals. Then, in the national finals in New York City, he beat an opponent who was much heavier. It took him only three rounds.

Discovering a New Religion

As he traveled more, Clay's inquiring mind was discovering the wider world of new ideas. While he was away at one of the boxing tournaments, Clay attended a meeting of a group called the Nation of Islam (NOI). His mother had raised him in the Baptist Church. This group was different, however, and he liked their message— that African Americans could be proud and independent and that they could stand on their own and didn't have to share space with white people who hated them. He admired the focus on living a clean life. Malcolm X, the main spokesperson for the Nation of Islam, later

> *"I'd never heard an athlete like him; he had no doubts, no fears, no second thoughts, not an ounce of false humility."*
>
> Sportswriter Dick Schaap

became Clay's inspiration and his mentor when he decided to change his religion. Many people living in the United States, black and white alike, found the NOI philosophy to be controversial. Malcolm X told African Americans to be proud because he thought they were the superior race. This went against what the leaders of the Civil Rights Movement—most of them African Americans—were saying. They felt that people of all races were to be treated equally. They were fighting for integration, or the mixing of races in daily life, instead of separating them.

Boxing Heroes

If young boys wanted African-American heroes to admire, they could find them in the boxing ring. Two beloved African-American boxing figures were Joe Louis and Jack Johnson. Clay's hero was boxer Sugar Ray Robinson. While in New York City in 1960, just before leaving for the Rome Olympics, Clay tried twice to meet Robinson. The first time, Robinson didn't show up. The second time, Clay waited all day outside Sugar Ray's bar in Harlem. Robinson finally arrived that night in a flashy car, but he didn't spend much time with the adoring young boxer. Clay was extremely disappointed. He vowed that, when he became famous, he would always have time for his fans.

Future Hopes

A young boy's dreams can come true with the right combination of hard work and perseverance. Clay's early skill as an athlete matured and developed until he turned in

Sugar Ray Robinson

Sugar Ray Robinson was a flamboyant boxer who drove a pink Cadillac. He was also a talented singer and dancer. His real name was Walker Smith Jr., but he used the ID card of a friend named Ray Robinson to enter a boxing tournament when he was 14 years old—two years younger than the permitted age. His style was called "sweet as sugar," which got him the nickname Sugar Ray. He earned Golden Gloves championships as an undefeated amateur. He served in the army in World War II, where he toured and put on boxing exhibitions with Joe Louis. After the war, he became welterweight champ in 1946 and middleweight champ in 1951 when he defeated the legendary "Raging Bull" Jake LaMotta. He was smaller than a heavyweight, but many sportswriters believed that "pound for pound" he was, at that time, the greatest boxer ever.

Sugar Ray Robinson is carried by a group of fellow boxers after being honored at the time of his retirement in 1965.

a gold-medal winning performance at the Olympics. His self-confidence and his rigorous training schedule also helped him. His coaches and trainers were also valuable supporters throughout his career as he pursued even greater dreams.

The Civil Rights Movement

Even though slavery was abolished in the 1860s, it took more than 100 years before the rights of African Americans were fully protected by law. In 1863, while the Civil War was still in progress, President Abraham Lincoln issued the Emancipation Proclamation. This declared the freedom of slaves in all the states that had joined the Confederate States of America. After the war, Lincoln pushed for the passage of the Thirteenth Amendment to the U.S. Constitution. The Thirteenth Amendment outlawed slavery in all states and territories. It was ratified in 1865.

Despite these legal changes, African Americans still didn't have full freedom, and they continued to suffer the effects of discrimination and racial persecution into the last half of the 20th century. Jim Crow laws, which restricted their rights and activities, were passed by many states in the South. While most northern states didn't have the same discriminatory laws as the South, African Americans in the North felt the effects of prejudice in education and finding jobs and housing.

The 1950s and 1960s were times of radical change as people tried to change laws to make life fair for the nation's black population. They did this through political pressure campaigns, drives to register African-American voters, and a series of demonstrations that included "sit-ins" in which people occupied places as a form of protest. Eloquent and inspirational black leaders such as Dr. Martin Luther King Jr. urged followers to fight in non-violent ways for more respect and equality.

The Civil Rights Movement pushed politicians to pass laws to protect people against discrimination on the basis of race, religion, and other factors. It has ultimately improved life for everyone in the United States.

Soldiers from the 101st Airborne Division of the U.S. Army escort nine African-American students into previously all-white Little Rock (Arkansas) Central High School in 1957.

CIVIL RIGHTS HIGHLIGHTS

1954 The U.S. Supreme Court declares that segregation in public schools is unconstitutional.

1955 African-American teenager Emmett Till is murdered in Mississippi for flirting with a white grocery clerk, and his killers go free.

1955 African-American bus passenger Rosa Parks is arrested for refusing to give up her seat to a white person in Montgomery, Alabama. This event sparked the Montgomery Bus Boycott, which will last for a year before the buses are finally desegregated.

1957 The Arkansas state governor blocks nine African-American students from attending a previously all-white high school in Little Rock, but President Dwight Eisenhower sends U.S. troops to protect their rights.

1960 African-American college students in Greensboro, North Carolina, start a non-violent sit-in at a Woolworth's lunch counter after being refused service. The protest continues for six months until they are finally served. This victory sparks similar sit-in protests throughout the South.

1961 Freedom Rides are organized by the Congress of Racial Equality as a way to test new laws prohibiting racial segregation on interstate transport. More than 1,000 student volunteers ride buses all over the South.

1963 Medgar Evers, secretary of the National Association for the Advancement of Colored People (NAACP) in Mississippi, is murdered. His killer is not convicted until 31 years later.

1963 The March on Washington attracts about 200,000 protesters, who hear civil rights leader Martin Luther King Jr. deliver his "I Have a Dream" speech.

1964 The federal government abolishes voting fees called poll taxes, that had made it difficult for impoverished African Americans to vote.

1964 The Civil Rights Act is passed to ban discrimination on the basis of race, religion, or national origin.

1964 Three civil rights workers—two white and one black—aiming to register black voters in Mississippi are arrested for speeding and later murdered by the terrorist Ku Klux Klan.

1965 Malcolm X, a political activist and controversial figure in the black nationalist and civil rights movements, is shot. He was allegedly killed by rivals in the black nationalist movement.

1965 Police in Selma, Alabama, use violence against a group of African-American protesters demanding voting rights.

1965 The Voting Rights Act is passed by the U.S. Congress, making it illegal to impose literacy tests, voting fees called poll taxes, and other obstacles that had reduced the number of black voters.

Chapter 3
Building a Career

When he returned to Kentucky after his Olympic triumph, Cassius Clay had to carefully plan his next move as he made the transition from amateur boxer to professional boxer. He was coming into the sport at a very good time, when boxing officials were trying to keep criminals and cheats away from the sport. In the years prior to Clay's time in the ring, the Mafia and other elements of organized crime paid off and controlled many fight managers and even some referees so that criminals could make money by betting on fights.

Refining the Talent

In the early 1960s, officials were trying to clean up boxing's reputation, and many of the crooks were in jail when Clay came on the scene. Clay was lucky to have the financial support of a group of wealthy businessmen in his hometown of Louisville. These businessmen formed the Louisville Sponsoring Group to manage him, providing him with a $10,000 signing bonus and a monthly salary in return for a share of his winnings. Clay immediately went out and bought his mother an expensive car.

There were also some disappointments when Clay returned to his life in the United States after his Olympic win. Even though the mayor of Louisville had told him that his gold medal was

the key to the city, the medal hadn't changed anything about his status as an African American in the South. Clay realized this after he went to lunch with a friend, and the waitress refused to serve them. The restaurant had a "whites-only" policy. No matter how famous and talented Clay was, it still didn't matter in the segregated South. This incident would bother him for years afterward.

In His Corner

A successful boxer needs a shrewd, talented, and committed team around him, and Clay was fortunate to have loyal and skilled cornermen and trainers. Finding the right trainer to bring out the best in this young boxer was a challenge. The Louisville Sponsoring Group's first response to that challenge—sending him to California to work with legendary boxer and trainer Archie Moore—didn't work out. Moore insisted that Clay perform such training camp chores as sweeping and dishwashing. Clay was opinionated and liked to do things his own way, and this routine didn't conform with his idea of what he should be doing in camp.

Next, the Louisville Sponsoring Group interviewed Angelo Dundee, who ran the 5th Street Gym in Miami. Years earlier, Dundee had been visiting Louisville when the then-15-year-old Cassius Clay phoned his hotel room to ask if they could meet and talk. Clay told him about the Golden Gloves awards he had already won and boasted that he was going to win at the Olympics in the future. Dundee was impressed by Clay's enthusiasm and answered his questions about training and techniques for three and a half hours.

LEGENDS OF THE RING

Rocky Marciano, whose real name was Rocco Marchegiano, was a short, stocky, and very tough heavyweight who was world champion from 1952 to 1956. As a boy growing up in Massachusetts, he had a passion for baseball. He learned to box in the army during World War II. Despite his late start, Marciano was good enough to make boxing his career. He retired undefeated in 1956, and died in a private plane crash in 1969 at age 45.

A statue of Rocky Marciano, "Champion of the World," in Italy.

Floyd Patterson is shown in a bout against Muhammad Ali in 1972.

Floyd Patterson, the youngest of 11 children, often got into trouble as a boy living in Brooklyn, New York. A judge sent him to reform school in upstate New York when he was 10 years old. After nearly two years at reform school he returned to the city and, at age 14, he learned to box. Just three years later, at age 17, he became the gold medalist in middleweight boxing at the 1952 Olympics. Patterson held his hands in front of his face higher than most boxers in what sportswriters called a "peekaboo" style. At 21, he was the youngest world heavyweight champ—a record later beaten by Mike Tyson—and the first Olympic gold medal boxer to win that title. He lost it to Ingemar Johansson in 1959 but, a year later, he was the first champion to regain the title. He fought two matches against Muhammad Ali in 1965 and 1972, losing both. The match in 1972 was his last. Floyd retired after that fight, at age 32.

Clay's managers picked Dundee to train the future champion, and Clay moved to Miami. Dundee was his head trainer from 1960 to 1981. He and Clay had a relationship that went beyond that of trainer and fighter. Dundee guided the boxer and even helped him with his poetry, but he didn't try to enforce strict rules or tell him how to handle his personal life. He let the fighter be himself, as both Cassius Clay and Muhammad Ali. Dundee's quick thinking and his never-give-up attitude helped Clay win, especially during difficult fights against Henry Cooper and Sonny Liston. "I'm proud to have been a friend of his," said Dundee. "He made me rich in so many ways during the most fun years I've ever had." As their relationship grew, Dundee enjoyed Muhammad Ali's exuberant antics—even such practical jokes as scaring Dundee by jumping out of a closet in Dundee's own hotel room.

Another valuable member of the training team was Drew Brown, nicknamed Bundini, who had experience as a cornerman for Sugar Ray Robinson prior to coming to Ali's camp. Brown had left school and joined the U.S. Navy at 13, before going to sea with the U.S. Merchant Marine. He was unique because he was a Jewish African American. He converted to Judaism when he married a Jewish woman.

> *"He was not just the life of the party; he was the party."*
>
> Angelo Dundee

A loyal employee from 1963 to 1981, he helped Ali write and often perform some of his best-known poems, including the one that included one of Ali's most famous lines: "Float like a butterfly, sting like a bee, your hands can't hit what your eyes can't see."

Reaching for the Top

Winning Olympic gold unlocked a few doors for the young Cassius Clay. One door that the gold medal did not open right away was the one leading to a shot at fighting the current heavyweight champion of the world, Sonny Liston. During the three years following Clay's Olympic win, he had to fight other well-known boxers to gain experience and develop a

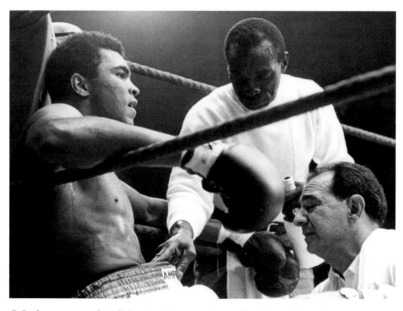

Muhammad Ali's trainer, Angelo Dundee (lower right), attends to the champ during a break in a 1966 fight in Germany.

reputation in the professional boxing world. In the first month of 1961, soon after he started training with Dundee in Miami, he fought and won three times. By the end of 1962, he was facing his 16th opponent—his old coach, Archie Moore. At 48 years old, Moore was a veteran who thought he could show Clay how it was done. By the fourth round, however, Clay had knocked him down three times. It was, as Clay had predicted, a knockout punch in the fourth that defeated Moore.

Boxing Meets Show Business

Even in the earlier years of his career— before changing his name to Muhammad Ali—Cassius Clay found ways of entertaining the public outside the ring with colorful and outrageous comments. This earned him one of his nicknames, "the Louisville Lip." Even as a teenager, he had been saying, "I am the greatest." In time, "The Greatest" became his self-styled nickname. Clay understood that boxing was show business as well as sports and that it could be entertaining as well as serious. He was only 19 years old when he met professional wrestler George Wagner while they were both at a radio station for interviews. Wagner called himself Gorgeous George, creating a vain character that audiences loved to hate. They paid good money to see him, but with the hope that his opponents would beat the daylights out of him. That was the way to sell tickets, he told Clay.

Clay took the wrestler's advice. Not only did he compose poetry with the help of Bundini Brown and others, but he also continued his

GORGEOUS GEORGE WAGNER: TURNING FIGHTING INTO ENTERTAINMENT

Nicknamed Gorgeous George for his long blond, curly hair, George Wagner was the most famous American professional wrestler during the 1940s and 1950s. He was one of the first to create a flamboyant character who made wrestling entertaining even before the actual fighting began. In a typical match, he made his entrance accompanied by music, wore flowing capes, and had the mat sprayed with disinfectant before he stepped into the ring.

Gorgeous George even got married in the ring. He liked to brag, and people bought tickets to the fight hoping to see him lose. In 1959, he promised to have his beautiful hair shaved off if he lost a match against his rival Whipper Billy Watson—and to the delight of the fans, that's exactly what happened.

This postcard of George Wagner includes a message from the wrestler: "Gorgeously Yours Gorgeous George."

> *"I called my opponents names and boasted of my abilities and beauty, and often predicted the round of my victory to infuriate them so they would make mistakes. Some may call this a trick, I just hoped it gave me an edge."*
>
> Muhammad Ali

habit of forecasting the round in which he would knock out his opponent. It was all part of his plan to confuse the competition. They didn't know whether he was crazy or just arrogant, but it made them want to punch him in the mouth.

The Skeptical Media

Sportswriters didn't know what to make of the boastful boxer and his unique, light-footed style that made a boxing match look more like ballet than fighting. Covering an arrogant young boxer who said he could stay pretty by avoiding punches wasn't typical fare for journalists used to interviewing men whose faces showed the beatings they took. His statements filled their newspaper columns and made for colorful TV and radio interviews, but journalists weren't sold on his big mouth. They wondered how successful he would be with his unorthodox

> *"Now here comes Cassius Clay popping off and abrasive and loud, and it was a jolt for a lot of sportswriters."*
>
> Robert Lipsyte, *The New York Times*

STICKS AND STONES

Nicknames were common in the world of boxing, but usually it was the writers, not the opponents, who made them up. Muhammad Ali had nicknames for most of the other boxers he met in the ring. Most of the time, the name-calling was lighthearted and referred to a boxer's appearance or behavior in the ring. Liston was the Bear, Joe Frazier the Gorilla, and Floyd Patterson the Rabbit. Leon Spinks was Dracula, and George Foreman was the Mummy. Ali once said that Canadian boxer George Chuvalo punched like a "washerwoman." Chuvalo went along with the joke and obliged by dressing up like an old woman with a scarf on his head for the media.

boxing style. They were used to quiet and more modest fighters, and they wanted to be the ones making up the descriptive prose. Yet here was Cassius Clay, who had recorded a record album of poems and monologues—all about how great he was—even before he won the heavyweight championship.

On His Way Up

Following his win over Archie Moore, Clay's promotional style paid off in a fight against Doug Jones in March 1963. Even though a newspaper strike prevented promoters from advertising the fight, Clay himself generated so much interest that New York's Madison Square Garden was sold out. Jones proved to be a tough opponent, and Clay's prediction that he would beat him in four rounds was wrong. It took 10 rounds for Clay to be declared the winner in a decision that was loudly booed by the crowd and disputed by many sportswriters.

> *"My plan was to dance, stay out of my opponent's reach, and use my wits as much as my fists."*
>
> Cassius Clay

That fight showed that Clay could handle a tough fighter even with his odd style that broke all the boxing rules. "My strategy was to be as scientific as I could when I fought," he said. His plan was to study his opponents' fighting style carefully and figure out how to counter their strong points. When he knew he had more stamina than an older boxer, he let his opponent wear himself out by throwing punches that Clay dodged during the early rounds. Clay then began his offensive assault in the later rounds.

In Clay's next fight, Henry Cooper endured some serious punishment before one of Cooper's punches caught Clay off guard and knocked him down. Clay was still woozy when he returned

> *"(Cassius Clay) always had a slight smile on his face. The public realized it over here: this is all a gimmick; this is clever; this is funny. And they laughed with him."*
>
> Henry Cooper

> *"(Cassius Clay) had a big heart, a good chin, fast feet, and fast hands. What more would you want?"*
>
> Henry Cooper

to the corner. Fortunately, his trainer, Angelo Dundee, noticed a small tear in one of Clay's boxing gloves. He drew the referee's attention to the tear, allowing more precious time for Clay to recover while the officials found a second pair of gloves. In the meantime, Dundee poured water over his boxer's head to clear his dizziness. By the start of the next round, Clay had renewed energy and came out punching until the fight was stopped due to Cooper's injuries.

Getting the Bear's Attention

Still undefeated after fighting some of the world's toughest boxers, Clay thought he was ready to challenge Sonny Liston, the heavyweight champion. Liston still wasn't paying any attention to Clay. Getting Liston to take notice involved stunts that got the media's attention and aroused the public's interest. Liston was already known as "the Bear," but Clay called him "the big ugly bear," as a way to goad Liston into fighting him. He had a bus painted with the words "World's most colorful boxer" and drove it to Liston's house in Denver in the middle of the night.

Clay's efforts to get Liston worked up enough to fight him had gone on for some

> *"I could use psychology on him—you know, needle him and work on his nerves so bad that I would have him beat before he ever got in the ring with me."*
>
> Cassius Clay on Sonny Liston

time. After the 1962 fight between Liston and then-champ Floyd Patterson, which Liston won by a knockout in the first round, Clay told journalists that he should be the one who was in the ring with Liston. He also uttered one of his famous poetic predictions: "Don't make me wait. I'll whup him in eight."

Of course, talking to the media was not as important as training hard for the fights. His trainer Angelo Dundee knew how to handle the young fighter with the big ego. He knew he couldn't give him direct orders. He had to use psychology and give the young boxer some freedom. "I tried to make Clay feel like he innovated everything," Dundee said.

> *"Who would have thought, when they came to the fight,*
> *That they'd witness the launching of a human satellite?*
> *Yes, the crowd did not dream, when they laid down their money,*
> *That they would see a total eclipse of the Sonny!*
> *I am the greatest!"*
>
> Cassius Clay on Sonny Liston

BEYOND THE BLUSTER

While "trash talking"—insulting and belittling opponents before competing against them—has long been part of the entertainment value in sports, Muhammad Ali brought it to a new level in boxing.

The name-calling was maintained right up to the start of the fight, and beyond. Ali used the official weigh-in, which took place a few days before the fight, as both a promotional opportunity and a way to anger his opponent. In some fights, he taunted the other boxer in the ring until the referee asked him to keep quiet.

The verbal sparring was a way to generate media attention and sell tickets to the fight. It was also a way for Ali to create an identity that would set him apart from the field and distinguish him from other African-American boxers.

When he wasn't sparring at the gym, Clay was running. He got out of bed at 5:00 A.M. for his first training session. The sight of a black man running at that hour prompted some people to think that he might be in trouble with the law. "I got calls from the police saying that there's some tall skinny black guy running, and did I know anything about it," said Dundee. He explained that the runner was a boxer in training.

"I set out to make him think what I wanted him thinking: that all I was was some clown."

Cassius Clay

SONNY LISTON

Sonny Liston was a world heavyweight champion boxer (1962–1964) known for his brutal punching style. He was the first contender ever to knock out a champion—Floyd Patterson—in the first round, a feat he repeated in a rematch with the former champ. He lost the title to Cassius Clay in 1964. One of 25 children born to a poor sharecropper in Arkansas, Liston left his abusive father to join his mother in St. Louis. He had little schooling, turned to robbery, and was sent to prison. There, the prison priest showed him how to box. His career included 50 wins and 4 losses. He died at 38, just 6 months after his last fight.

Clay vs Liston, 1964

Finally, Sonny Liston agreed to fight the young contender. The fight would take place in Miami on February 25, 1964. People were betting seven to one against Clay, as most people believed the boastful young fighter would be beaten badly. After all, Liston was a skilled boxer with a reputation for being a dangerous and menacing fighter.

People didn't think Clay could win, but they were definitely interested in knowing what the outcome would be, especially after so much boasting. The fighter used that bragging tactic over and over during his career to draw

> *"The only thing at which Clay can beat Liston is reading the dictionary."*
>
> Jim Murray, *Los Angeles Times*

attention to the matches and sell tickets. A week before the Liston fight, the Beatles were in Miami as part of their U.S. concert tour. They visited Clay while he was working out at his gym, and photographers captured him pretending to knock all four of them down with one punch.

The Fight Begins

If Clay was nervous on the night of the fight, he didn't show it. In the first round, he made Liston look clumsy and lumbering as he danced away from Liston's powerful punches. He also managed to land a few jabs of his own on the surprised champion.

In Miami to train for his upcoming fight against Sonny Liston, Cassius Clay works the crowd during a parade in December 1963.

His first comment to the reporters seated near the ring was "Eat your words!" He had proven them wrong.

In the second round, Clay delivered a series of combination blows to wear Liston down and, by round three, he had opened a cut under Liston's eye.

Suddenly, in the fourth round, Clay's right eye started to burn and his sight became blurred. He was blinded by a stinging substance that some have suggested might have been some kind of liniment or ointment from Liston's gloves.

"Cut off my gloves!" Clay begged his trainer, Dundee, indicating his desire to put an end to the bout. Dundee shouted back, "This is the big one, daddy ... we're not quitting now." And, in one of the most crucial decisions of his career, Dundee refused to let his man give up. Instead, he swabbed Clay's eye with water to dilute the stinging substance.

Reluctantly, Clay came out of his corner for the fifth round and stumbled around taking punches from Liston. He was blinking a lot and could not see well enough to deliver

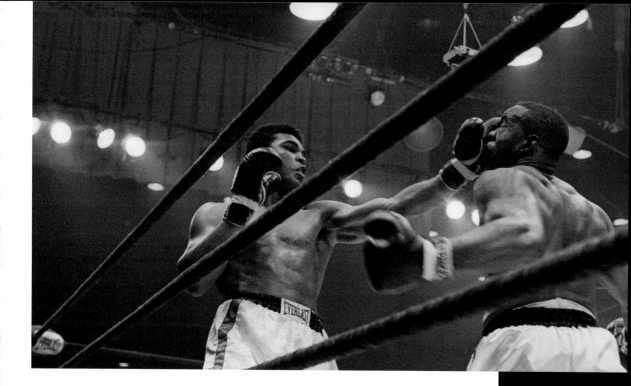

any accurate blows himself. The outcome of the fight didn't look good for the challenger, but he managed to survive the round.

In the sixth, Clay's eyesight had improved, and he was once again dancing around and delivering punches. The fight seemed to be pretty competitive at this point, and viewers were looking forward to a few more rounds. Shockingly, when the bell rang for the start of the seventh round, Liston refused to come out of his corner. Complaining to his cornermen of a shoulder injury, the champ had given up, and Clay was pronounced the winner.

Clay was the world heavyweight champion! His first comment to the reporters seated near the ring was "Eat your words!" He had proven them wrong. Clay's faith in himself and his careful training and research of Liston's fighting style had earned him the heavyweight title.

Cassius Clay lands a punch against Sonny Liston in the sixth round during their fight in 1964.

Chapter 4
The Man Behind the Gloves

Sports fans expect athletes to perform on the field of play. They rarely expect to hear their heroes' opinions about anything but sports. This was particularly true in the 1950s and 1960s, when athletes were expected to be seen but not heard—unlike athletes today. Muhammad Ali was different. He showed people of all races that African Americans can be proud of their culture and their identity, and be vocal in expressing that pride. He also supported the movement for civil rights for all Americans. He backed up his words with actions. That made him a hero to many, even beyond the sports arena.

A Different Breed

At the time of his 1964 fight with Sonny Liston, there was talk of Ali's interest in the Muslim faith and in the Nation of Islam in particular. Word got out that the young Cassius Clay had been seen in the company of members of the controversial Nation of Islam (NOI). The fight promoter worried that such news would hurt the revenue generated by the fight, and he threatened to cancel it. As a compromise, the promoter got Clay to agree not to announce his conversion to Islam until after the fight.

Many of the ideas preached by members of the Nation of Islam—sometimes called Black Muslims—were different from those of mainstream Islam, particularly as it was practiced throughout the rest of the world. NOI directed their appeal specifically to African Americans, preaching that the black race was the original and superior race. They believed in creating a separate African-American state and disagreed with civil rights activists who fought for integration and equality among people of all races. Elijah Muhammad, their leader when Clay joined the group in 1964, had been jailed in the 1940s for failing to register for the military draft and instructing his followers that they should not serve in World War II.

Not eager to make his interest in Islam public, the young Cassius Clay (shown here, left center, in dark suit) sneaked into Nation of Islam (NOI) meetings. Here he is shown listening to an address by NOI leader Elijah Muhammad.

THE NATION OF ISLAM

The Nation of Islam (NOI) is an African-American group tha
many of the beliefs of Islam, but also had teachings that are
from those of mainstream Islam. Wallace Fard—who later ac
Muhammad to his name—founded it in Detroit in 1930. Th
are related to the politics of race and identity for African Am
sought to instill a pride in being black that most African Ame
rarely felt.

In addition to the political side of the NOI, the group's te
controversial compared to those of Christianity, Judaism, an
Islam. According to NOI teachings, the black race is the orig
race and is superior to all others. Wallace maintained that a
scientist named Yakub created a dishonest and dominant w
Wallace's followers believed that he was the long-awaited M
Savior, foretold by the Jews, and the Mahdi, or redeemer, of
NOI members are told that a Mother Plane or Wheel, simila
described in visions in the Bible, has been circling Earth for
After the Nation's second leader, Elijah Muhammad, died in
group basically split in half. Elijah's son Wallace became the
a more moderate group that shifted toward traditional Musl
Another member, Louis Farrakhan, became leader of the gro
revived, and continues to bear, the name *Nation of Islam.*

Islamic Inspiration

One person associated with the NOI who grew
close to Clay was civil rights activist Malcolm
X. Malcolm and his family visited Clay at his
Miami training camp before the Liston fight.
Malcolm continued to support Clay and inspire
him to follow Islam. By this time, Malcolm had
broken away from the NOI because of a falling
out between him and spiritual leader Elijah
Muhammad.

Soon after his win over Liston to become the heavyweight champion, Clay announced that he had converted to Islam from the Baptist faith in which he was raised. He became a member of the Nation of Islam. The spiritual leader Elijah Muhammad gave Cassius a new name: Muhammad Ali.

At the time, Ali's opinions and his race were enough to make many people hate him. He was African-American, Muslim, and against the war in Vietnam, which made people think he was unpatriotic. It would be a few years before people would accept that the freedoms to choose one's religion and to speak one's views were as important to protect for someone like Ali as it was for others with less radical views. In the turbulent 1960s, however, politics, life styles, and even personal appearance could have a polarizing effect.

Ali had his admirers from all races. He was also unpopular, mainly with Americans who were unhappy with other changes going on around them. Ali's beliefs deeply affected his career and his personal life.

Muslim Life

Ali's decision to adopt a new religion affected his life in ways he had not expected. A few months after his first fight with Liston, Ali got married for the first time, to waitress Sonji Roi. She was reluctant to adopt Muslim dress codes and practices, however, and their marriage ended 17 months later.

After his win against Liston, Ali made a highly publicized trip to Africa with stops in Nigeria, Egypt, and Ghana. He toured

MALCOLM X

Malcolm X was born Malcolm Little in Nebraska. He was a brilliant speaker and activist for African-American rights. His father Earl was a civil rights activist and Baptist minister. His opinions resulted in death threats from white supremacist groups, and it was rumored that it was members of such a group who killed Earl when Malcolm was just six years old.

Although Malcolm was an excellent student in junior high school, he later dropped out and became a petty criminal. While serving seven years for burglary, he studied the teachings of the Nation of Islam (NOI). On parole in 1952, he began calling himself Malcolm X, saying that Little was his slave name. He joined the NOI and was soon appointed chief spokesperson for the group. By the time he began his association with Muhammad Ali, tensions had developed between Malcolm and the NOI, particularly with leader Elijah Muhammad.

On March 8, 1964, Malcolm announced his departure from the NOI, based on his feeling that the Nation was bound by rigid religious teachings. He also wanted to work closely with more traditional civil rights leaders and have a positive effect on the lives and thinking of larger numbers of African Americans.

On February 21, 1965, while preparing to address a crowd in New York City, he was shot and killed by men believed to be associated with the NOI. No reason for the NOI to kill Malcolm was ever discovered. Conspiracy theories surrounding his assassination covered everyone from drug dealers to the FBI.

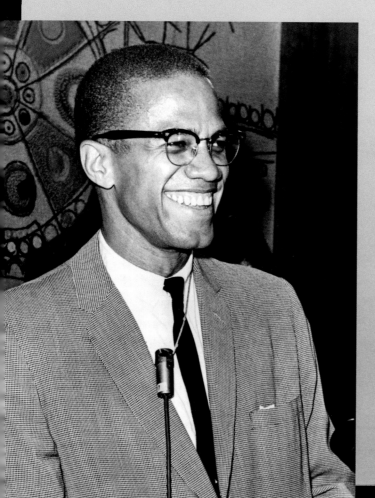

Malcolm X in March 1964, about a year before his death.

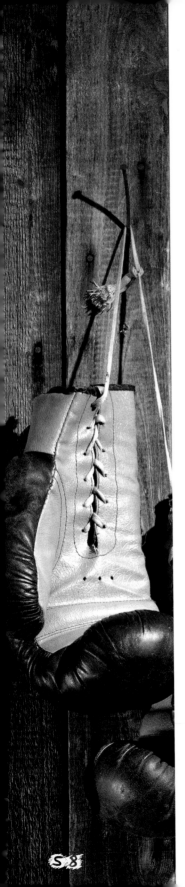

hospitals, put on boxing exhibitions, and met politicians such as the president of Ghana, Kwame Nkrumah. His entourage included his brother Rahman—who had changed his name from Rudy when he also converted to Islam—and Herbert Muhammad, Elijah's son. This trip would be a great opportunity for the Nation of Islam to spread their message through their most magnetic convert. The trip also gave Ali new insight into his heritage as an African American. He wore native clothes and told his fans that he would love to hold a boxing match in Africa. His supporters—children and adults—turned out by the thousands, calling him "king of the world."

Rejecting Malcolm

Before Ali's trip to Africa, Elijah Muhammad asked Ali not to associate with Malcolm X now that Malcolm had broken away from the Nation of Islam. Ali agreed, and he publicly ignored Malcolm when he happened to meet him in a hotel in Ghana. Malcolm was also touring Africa at the same time and had made a pilgrimage to Mecca in Saudi Arabia, considered a holy city by devout Muslims. Ali would say later that snubbing Malcolm was one of his greatest regrets. While Ali was on top of the world, his former friend and mentor was under increasing threat of violence. In 1965, only a few months after seeing Ali in Africa, Malcolm X's house was firebombed, and he needed guards to protect his family from harm. A week later, Malcolm X was assassinated while appearing at a rally in New York City. He was 39 years old.

A decade later, Ali would follow Malcolm's route to Sunni Islam, a more traditional form of the religion. In the meantime, he maintained his association with the NOI. In 1966, after the contract expired with Ali's original financial backers, the Louisville Sponsoring Group NOI leader Elijah Muhammad appointed his son Herbert to be the boxer's personal manager. Herbert would manage Ali's business affairs until the early 1990s.

ISLAM

With more than 1.5 billion followers, Islam, which means "surrender," is the second-largest religion in the world after Christianity. People who follow Islam are called Muslims. Muslims believe that their religion began with a man named Muhammad, who was a merchant living in Mecca (now part of Saudi Arabia) more than 1,400 years ago.

Muhammad was considered to have been a prophet who heard the word of Allah (God). After his death, the teachings were collected in a book called the Qu'ran (sometimes spelled *Koran*). Muslims believe that there is one God, and central figures in Judaism and Christianity, such as Abraham, Moses, and Jesus, were prophets as well. Islam consists of several branches, the largest being Sunni Islam, with about 75 percent of all Muslims. Orthodox Muslims follow practices that touch their daily lives, such as prayer rituals and observing restrictions on diet and clothing. Certain foods such as pork are forbidden, and women are encouraged to dress modestly. The largest Muslim countries are Indonesia and Pakistan. Islam is also the predominant religion in many countries in Africa, Asia, and the Arab countries of the Middle East.

Defending the Title

Once a boxer earns a world championship, there is no shortage of contenders who want to take it away from him. First in line was the former champion Sonny Liston. Ali wanted a rematch to prove that his win wasn't just a fluke. The fight was scheduled for November 1964, nine months after Ali had won the first event. This time, now that he knew what a skilled boxer Ali was, Liston trained much harder. Just three days before the fight, however, Ali had emergency surgery for a hernia, and the fight was postponed until the following year. Liston was disappointed, but he managed a rare joke: "If he'd stop all that hollering, he wouldn't have a hernia."

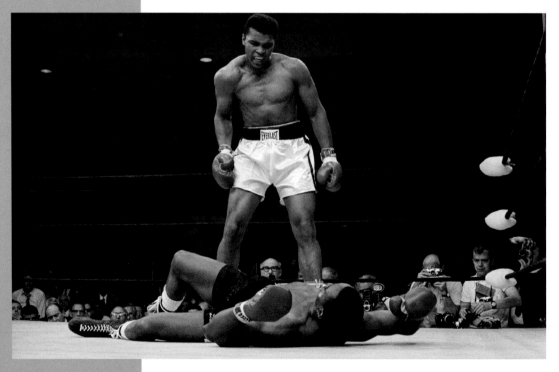

In this classic photograph from the second Ali-Liston fight, Ali is shown standing over Sonny Liston, taunting him and yelling at him to get up.

The rematch with Liston was finally held on May 25, 1965, in Lewiston, Maine. The fight was held in a small arena. But the promoters knew that, on top of ticket sales, they could profit from people who paid to see the fight through a special broadcast on closed-circuit TV at their local movie theaters. Millions more listened over the radio. Rumors circulated that there might be violence at the match, so the arena increased security and had more police officers.

Once more, people believed Liston would be the winner. In the first round, however, Ali planted two heavy punches that knocked Liston to the floor. The punch that seemed most effective was something Ali called the "anchor punch." Ali yelled at Liston to get up and fight, as he didn't want to win so soon, but the referee declared Ali the winner. For many years, people questioned how Liston could have gone down so quickly, and stayed down. One theory was that Liston "took a dive" as part of a "fix" by a criminal organization. Another theory was that Liston said that Ali and the fight were out of control and that he wanted no more to do with either. Others thought that Liston was possibly affected by drugs or alcohol and couldn't fight.

Patterson in Las Vegas, 1965

Boxers often represent something larger than themselves, whether it's a country or a racial or ethnic group. When former world champion Floyd Patterson stepped forward to challenge Ali following Ali's defense of his crown against Liston, he saw himself as the Christian hero defeating the Muslim. This time it was

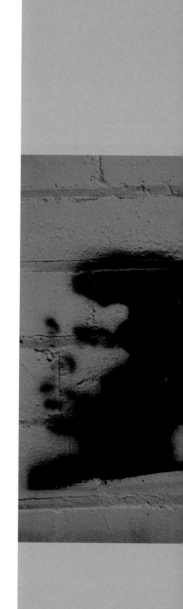

Patterson who did more entertaining trash talking. His interviews in sports magazines made it clear that for him the fight was a moral crusade, and that his side was the right side to be on. He insisted on calling Ali by his original birth name to show his contempt for Ali's new name, his views on race and politics, and his religious identity.

Patterson had lost badly—twice—to Liston. However, he was also an Olympic gold medalist like Ali, with a long list of wins as a professional. He liked to say that he may have fallen down more than some boxers, but he also got up more, too.

When the two men finally met in a Las Vegas, Nevada, boxing ring in November 1965, Ali was the favorite with odds of seven to one. In the first rounds, Ali danced around as usual, testing Patterson's reflexes with fake punches and jabs. As he tried to hit his speedy opponent, Patterson got injured himself. "I took a swing at him and missed, and I got a muscle spasm, and after that I could not swing without great pain," said Patterson.

Round after round, Ali used verbal taunts as well as punches against his slower rival. To rile him up, Ali kept calling Patterson names and demanding that he call him "Ali" and not "Clay." Ali avoided delivering a knockout punch, and Patterson grew more and more battered but would not let the referee stop the fight earlier. Finally, in the 12th round, Ali's jabs turned to a barrage of punches to the head, and the officials declared the fight over to protect Patterson from serious injury. Ali had not only survived the latest challenger, but triumphed decisively.

Anti-War Beliefs

As a Muslim, Ali was against serving in the U.S. military. In particluar, he opposed the Vietnam War for many reasons. A few years earlier, he had registered for the military, as young men were expected to do. But he was classified as ineligible because of his poor scores on the written test. As he would later say, "I only said I was the greatest, not the smartest." In 1966, with more troops needed for battle in Vietnam, entrance standards to the military were revised to include more men. Ali's status was changed, and he became eligible for the draft. This meant he was part of a pool of men who were considered potential soldiers, and the government could call them up to serve.

Ali declared that he considered himself a conscientious objector, which is defined as a person who claims the right to refuse to perform military service on moral grounds that include religion and other personally held moral beliefs. He told officials that if he was drafted, he would refuse to serve in the military based on his objection to war in general, and to the war in Vietnam in particular.

Officials had told him that because of his fame, serving in the military would be easier for him. He wouldn't have to go into battle. Instead, he could put on exhibition fights and visit the troops, just as the great boxer Joe Louis had done in World War II. Still, he disagreed and wanted to stand up for what he believed in. He knew the penalty for refusing to go to war could be a jail term. Even so, he believed that the war was wrong, and he was willing to suffer the consequences, whether it was jail or a fine.

"I ain't got no quarrel with them Vietcong. No Vietcong ever called me nigger."

Muhammad Ali

> *"They were angry with him. And I remember thinking, this must be a pretty strong guy, facing the wrath of the U.S. government, facing possible imprisonment, facing possible exile from the fight game itself."*
>
> Canadian boxer George Chuvalo

Ahead of the Curve

Ali's opposition to the war, and his willingness to back up his beliefs with words and actions, were several steps ahead of the majority of the American population. In the mid-1960s, most Americans believed that the United States should keep fighting until it won whatever war the nation was fighting. Only weeks before Ali's refusal to be inducted into the military, Nobel Peace Prize winner Dr. Martin Luther King Jr. had delivered a speech in New York that explained why the United States should get out of the war in Vietnam. As a result, King was labeled a traitor by the government and by many in the media. Major newspapers stated that he should stick to issues such as civil rights. King argued, however, that they couldn't fix the problems between the black and white populations in the country when they were spending so much money and attention on the war.

Meanwhile, Ali's career as a boxer suffered greatly because of his anti-war stance. The public—and boxing officials—were angry with his refusal to become a soldier. Ali was

supposed to defend his title against challenger
Ernie Terrell in Chicago, but the Illinois Boxing
Commission would not permit the fight until Ali
apologized in public for his anti-war remarks.
Ali refused.

In 1966, Ali left the country for his next few
fights because of increasing hostility against
him. He fought against George Chuvalo in
Canada, and had a rematch with Henry Cooper
in the United Kingdom. He won both fights.
He continued to travel, winning a bout against
European champion Karl Mildenberger, who
had not been defeated in the ring for four years.
Back home in the United States toward the
end of 1966 and into 1967, he defeated more
challengers and introduced more dazzling
moves and vicious verbal attacks in the ring
before sometimes hostile audiences. In Houston,
he showed off fancy footwork he called the Ali
Shuffle before dropping Cleveland Williams
three times in the fourth round. In the same
city, Ali punished Ernie Terrell through 15
rounds and taunted him during the ugly fight,
demanding to be told, as he had with Floyd

> *"No one who has any concern for the
> integrity and life of America today can
> ignore the present war. If America's
> soul becomes totally poisoned, part of
> the autopsy must read: Vietnam."*
>
> Dr. Martin Luther King Jr.

Patterson, "What's my name?" since Terrell still called him "Clay." In March 1967, Ali defeated Zora Folley in the seventh round in what would be his last fight for several years. He was booed by the crowd, and the announcer called him "part clown, part bicycle rider." Nonetheless, with an undefeated record of 29 wins, Ali was still on top of the boxing world, but he knew that was about to change.

The Boxer and the Broadcaster

One journalist and broadcaster who befriended Ali and interviewed him dozens of times throughout his career was Howard Cosell. Despite their very different backgrounds,

Muhammad Ali (right) relaxes with friends in his hotel room in Toronto, Canada, before his fight with George Chuvalo in March 1966. He is pointing to a newspaper headline to show that he is not the only person protesting the Vietnam War.

Ali and the opinionated sportscaster made for a colorful combination. Ali would tease Cosell about his wig and claim on-air that the journalist needed him more than he needed Cosell. Cosell was supportive of Ali's religious conversion, however, and was one of the first journalists to use his new name. Many writers and boxers continued to call him "Cassius Clay." When Cosell died in 1995, Ali said:

> *"I have been interviewed by many people, but I enjoyed interviews with Howard the best. I hope to meet him one day in the hereafter. I can hear Howard now saying, 'Muhammad, you're not the man you used to be.'"*

Arrogant, pompous, obnoxious, vain, cruel, verbose, a show off. I have been called all of these. Of course, I am.

Howard Cosell

HOWARD COSELL

Howard Cosell gave sports journalism a new twist with his controversial opinions and hard-nosed reporting skills during his radio and TV career, which began in the mid-1950s. Cosell was Jewish, and his birth name was Cohen. Like many in the entertainment business, he changed his name to something that was less "Jewish sounding." Before switching to broadcasting, he was a lawyer. He spent 14 years as a commentator on ABC's *Monday Night Football* and covered other high-profile sporting events. These included boxing matches, many of them fought by Muhammad Ali.

Cosell's trademark nasal Brooklyn accent, his cigar, his emphatic, abrupt style of speech, and his wig made him the most recognized journalist in the United States. At a time when most sportswriters were boosters for local teams, rather than investigative reporters and critics, Cosell stood out. Instead of acting as a cheerleader, he reported on issues such as corruption or the unfair treatment of athletes. His catchphrase was "I'm just telling it like it is." And he did.

Champ Arrested

In 1967, Ali finally received his draft notice, instructing him to appear at the induction center in Houston to receive his orders. After refusing several times to step forward when his name was called out, he was arrested and eventually found guilty on charges of evading the draft. He was sentenced to five years in jail and fined $10,000. Ali was prepared to serve time in prison for his beliefs, if that was what he had to do. He was allowed to be out on bail while his lawyers worked on an appeal, but it meant that his career was in jeopardy. He had to be stronger than he had ever been in the ring.

A medic treats the wounds of a young Marine in Hue City, South Vietnam, in 1968.

THE VIETNAM WAR

The Vietnam War was a conflict fought in Southeast Asia primarily between North and South Vietnam. In 1945, leader Ho Chi Minh declared North Vietnam to be an independent country, and his government was supported by communist countries such as China and the Soviet Union. In the 1950s and 1960s, the United States, France, and other anti-communist nations supported South Vietnam. Ho created a fighting force called the Vietcong and attempted to take over South Vietnam. The United States stepped up its military presence in Vietnam to stop the spread of communism. The United States had forces in Vietnam since the mid-1950s, but 1959 is the year when U.S. involvement began on a large scale.

The United States was further drawn into the war in 1964, when a U.S. warship became engaged in conflict with North Vietnamese ships in a confrontation known as the Gulf of Tonkin incident. The United States started bombing heavily and sending more of its troops overseas. The American public began to shift in favor of ending the war after the January 1968 Tet Offensive, which was a huge surprise attack by the Vietcong on targets in South Vietnam, including the American Embassy.

Following his election in 1968, American President Richard M. Nixon promised to begin bringing troops home. But, under his administration, the United States began bombing neighboring Cambodia. In addition to the intensity of a conflict that was robbing the nation of its young people, dividing the nation politically, and raising serious doubts as to its being winnable, other events began to eat away at the solidarity of the American people behind the war effort.

One such event was the massacre of hundreds of unarmed civilians in My Lai, South Vietnam, by U.S. troops in 1968. Another was the publishing, in 1971, of secret government memos in the *New York Times*. These papers exposed lies that had been created by the government during the Vietnam era. This report, popularly known as "The Pentagon Papers," contributed to a massive increase in public mistrust of the government's handling of the war.

U.S. combat troops were all withdrawn after a peace accord was signed in 1974. A year later, the South surrendered to the North after an invasion to unify the country. More than two million Americans served in Vietnam, and about 58,000 U.S. troops died in the conflict.

Chapter 5
Fighting His Way Back

Muhammad Ali had faced some fierce competitors in the boxing ring, but the U.S. government proved to be his strongest opponent yet in the battle over his anti-war beliefs. Would Ali eventually face a prison term for refusing to join the military? He had to wait several years before he knew the answer.

Fighting the Feds

Even though he was convicted on the charges of evading the draft, Ali was released on bail while his lawyers appealed the court decision. His case eventually reached the U.S. Supreme Court before a final ruling emerged, but that process took years.

Stripping Ali of the title he had struggled for and banning him from boxing were devastating blows to this athlete in his prime.

> *"What the government did to this man was inhuman and illegal under the Fifth and Fourteenth amendments. Nobody says a damned word about the professional football players who dodged the draft. But Muhammad was different; he was black and he was boastful."*
>
> Broadcaster Howard Cosell

While he waited to see where the court case would take him, Ali suffered another serious setback. Boxing authorities immediately stripped him of his world heavyweight title and suspended his boxing license. He was unable to box in any state in the United States.

Boxer in Exile

Stripping Ali of the title he had struggled for and banning him from boxing were devastating blows to this athlete in his prime. He had been offered chances to fight outside the United States, but he was unable to go because his passport had been taken away from him as one of the terms of being allowed out on bail.

To support his family in the years when he was exiled from the sport, he opened a restaurant called Champburger. He traveled frequently to make speeches on Islamic teachings to college students and other groups. Ali had more responsibilities now, too. He had remarried in 1967 to Belinda Boyd. She converted to Islam, and she changed her name to Khalilah Ali. The couple started a family when Ali was banned from boxing, and over the years they had four children: Maryum (born 1968), twins Rasheda and Jamillah (born 1970), and Muhammad Jr. (born 1972).

Now that there was no longer an undisputed world champion, boxing officials planned a tournament of the high-ranking boxers to decide who would take the title. Undefeated Joe Frazier met Jimmy Ellis in the ring in Madison Square Garden in New York for the final fight, with Frazier knocking out Ellis in the fifth round. Meanwhile, Ali didn't let the media forget him. He attended boxing matches as a spectator and, after they were over, he always claimed that he was the one who should be in the ring.

Back in the Ring

With attitudes changing about the Vietnam War by the end of the 1960s, Muhammad Ali's protest was seen in a more positive light. Many more Americans agreed with him that the United States should get out of the Vietnam War. Finally, in September 1970, the Supreme Court ruled that the New York State Athletic Commission had unlawfully suspended Ali's boxing license. After all, they had handed out boxing licenses to other men who had been arrested for crimes. Why should Ali's case be any different? Once the New York case was settled, the door was open for Ali to get his license reinstated across the nation.

This decision was what Ali had been waiting for. It meant that the boxing associations had to let him box again. Ali still had the elaborate

THE ANTI-WAR MOVEMENT

Most Americans supported their country's fight against communist forces in North Vietnam at the beginning of the United States' active involvement in the Vietnam War in 1959. At first, anti-war protesters were a small group of students and peace activists. When the United States began bombing North Vietnam in 1965, the students' message attracted labor unions, teachers, church leaders, and many others. Protest marches grew in size as more Americans believed the United States should not be part of the conflict. By 1969, a march on Washington attracted 500,000 protesters.

Military police stand watch over a group of of anti-war protesters in Washington, D.C., in 1967.

As the fighting grew more intense, public opinion shifted. People questioned the morality and the cost of the war in terms of money and the lives of the American soldiers and the Vietnames. By the end, more than 2 million U.S. soldiers had served in Vietnam, 58,000 of them were killed and thousands more wounded, and the war had cost billions of dollars.

Young men were drafted at random through a lottery system. Men burned their draft registration cards in protest, and many fled to Canada to escape punishment. Civil rights leaders such as Dr. Martin Luther King Jr. spoke out against the war. Increasing numbers of politicians also spoke out against the war as part of their campaigns for elective office. Protests continued on college campuses, with violent reactions from authorities. In 1970, at Kent State University, Ohio National Guardsmen fired on non-violent protesters, killing four people. This and other confrontations further fanned the flames of protest.

In 1970, events such as moving the conflict into Cambodia and the leak of the secret "Pentagon Papers" into the media created more outrage and mistrust of the U.S. government. More and more Americans were becoming dissatisfied with the war. Public pressure, and the likelihood that the United States could not win the Vietnam War, resulted in the withdrawal of U.S. troops by 1974.

crested belt that boxers receive when they win a championship. He thought of himself as the world heavyweight champ even though it had been more than three years since he was allowed to defend his title.

After the long period away from the ring, Ali was anxious to begin his quest to reach the top once more. Before he could meet the new champ, Joe Frazier, he had to get some practice against other fighters. Only a month after he was allowed to box again, in October 1970, Ali fought Jerry Quarry in Atlanta. Boxing promoters were happy to have the colorful boxer who attracted such attention—and sold tickets—back in the ring.

Not everyone wanted to see Ali return. He still inspired hatred, particularly in the South, where some spoke out against Ali and hoped he would be beaten by Quarry. Ali rose above the commotion, however, and defeated Quarry in three rounds.

Beyond the Bluster

Name-calling and hyped-up chatter before a fight were standard practices for Ali as a way to grab attention and sell tickets. His outrageous comments rarely reflected how he really felt about his fellow boxers, however. After the matches, he was gracious in victory and ready to compliment other fighters. He once praised his Canadian opponent George Chuvalo, who went 15 rounds with him without a knockout. Ali said, "George's head is the hardest thing I ever punched." He would sometimes use another colorful line to describe his opponents

> *"Of all the men I fought, Sonny Liston was the scariest, George Foreman was the most powerful, Floyd Patterson was the most skilled as a boxer. But the roughest and toughest was Joe Frazier. He brought out the best in me, and the best fight we fought was in Manila."*
>
> Muhammad Ali

after a fight, by saying "He hit me so hard, it shook my kinfolk back in Africa."

Many people believe that Ali's pre-fight insults and lighthearted trash talk went too far with his greatest opponent Joe Frazier. In fact, Frazier had been good to Ali, loaning him money during his exile from boxing and actively lobbying to reinstate Ali's boxing license. Once they had set the date to fight in 1971, Frazier agreed to go along with any publicity stunts Ali could dream up. Nonetheless, Frazier and his family were hurt by Ali's taunts, many of which deeply cut the boxer known as Smokin' Joe.

Ali had called Frazier ignorant, even though Ali had failed the same test as Frazier when they registered for the military. Ali called him the white man's champ, and an Uncle Tom—at the time, one of the worst insults for an African American. Finally, Ali's taunts about Frazier's appearance, calling him a gorilla, were the kind of stereotypical racist comments that were increasingly unacceptable from anyone, let alone another man of the same race. Frazier

> *"The message that the bigmouth sent out was that I was a caveman with gloves, too stupid to get out of the way of the punches."*
>
> Joe Frazier

said that his children were taunted at school because of the insults.

Years later, Ali made a public apology to Frazier: "I said a lot of things in the heat of the moment that I shouldn't have said. Called him names I shouldn't have called him. I apologize for that. I'm sorry. It was all meant to promote the fight."

The Fight of the Century—Ali vs Frazier, 1971

Ali was ready to face Joe Frazier, the current heavyweight champion, and regain his title. At least that's what he thought. Ali had prepared thoroughly for the fight, but Frazier was a powerful opponent. The event was wildly popular, with 300 million people watching via closed-circuit TV.

Never before had two such champions—the current one and the former one—met in the ring. Both had been unbeaten in their careers, so this would be the deciding match, dubbed the Fight of the Century. The fight was set for

"I made that New Year's resolution (1971) that I was going to dust that butterfly off. I was going to clip his wings...I wanted to close his lips."

Joe Frazier

Joe Frazier (left) and Muhammad Ali engage in a shouting, finger-pointing match during the contract ceremony for their March 1971 Fight of the Century.

UNCLE TOM

Calling a black person, particularly a man, an "Uncle Tom" is an insult suggesting he is meek and subservient to white people he believes to be his superiors. In fact, the name comes from an 1852 novel, called *Uncle Tom's Cabin*, by Harriet Beecher Stowe. The novel spotlighted the evils of slavery, and Uncle Tom was portrayed as a very strong character who refused to betray some runaway slaves and is killed because of his disobedience. Later plays based on the book made Uncle Tom a foolish and weak character, an inaccurate portrayal that was the origin of the negative view today.

A scene from the book Uncle Tom's Cabin *showing Tom with Eva, whom he saved from drowning, as depicted by British painter Edwin Longsden Long in 1866.*

March 1971, in New York. Each fighter would receive $2.5 million which, back then, was an astounding sum of money. The two boxers put on a thrilling show that didn't disappoint the fans. They were evenly matched during the first rounds. Frazier was much shorter than Ali, but he was fierce and planted his powerful left hook to drop Ali to the floor in the 15th and final round. Ali got up and made it to the end of the bout, but Frazier was declared the winner by the judges and won by decision.

For the first time in his career, Ali was on the losing side. Despite the loss, he refused to show disappointment. He was still a popular figure, and he called himself the People's Champ.

Winning the Court Battle

Ali was soon to win a different kind of fight in his pursuit of freedom of religion and speech. In June 1971, the Supreme Court ruled that the government had not properly made its case against Ali and reversed his conviction for refusing to serve in the military. With the threat of spending time in jail lifted off his shoulders, he was free to pursue his dream of recapturing the world heavyweight title.

Shaping Up to Win

For the next year and a half, Ali fought—and won—10 times against opponents in the United States and other countries, including Canada, Ireland, and Japan. In March 1973, he showed just how determined and courageous he was during a San Diego fight with Ken Norton in which he was the five-to-one favorite. Norton had not fought any major title holders and didn't seem to be a threat, but he landed a punch that broke Ali's jaw early in the fight.

Ali refused to quit, but the injury put him on the defensive. He stayed in the ring for all 12 rounds, spending much of the time trying to protect his face. Norton, who was considered the underdog, scored an upset win by decision. After the fight, Ali was taken directly to the hospital for surgery. Six months later, he came back to beat Norton narrowly in their rematch.

Several months before their September 1973 rematch, Muhammad Ali kiddingly points out the broken jaw Ken Norton gave him during their first fight in March. Ali beat Norton in the rematch.

Ali vs Frazier Rematch, January 1974

While Ali was building up his strength for a rematch against the first man to beat him in his professional career, Frazier had lost the heavyweight championship to George Foreman. Foreman had beaten Frazier for the title by knocking him down an amazing six times in just two rounds.

In the complicated process of pairing up contenders to arrive at a single world heavyweight champ, Ali had to face Foreman before he could get his title back. First, however, Ali wanted to avenge his humiliating loss against Frazier—the first of his career. So, even though his second fight against Frazier wasn't a title match, it was still very important to Ali's pride.

The two fighters' competitiveness was clear days before the January 28 fight, when they were both interviewed on a TV sports program.

Seated beside each other for the show, they began with taunts and name-calling, then Frazier wrestled Ali to the ground. They were both fined $5,000 for their misconduct.

After 12 rounds of pummelling, the rematch ended with a unanimous decision for Ali. Now they had each won a fight. Tied at 1-1, they would meet again the following year for the deciding match.

Rumble in the Jungle—Ali vs Foreman, Zaire, October 1974

In his quest to win back the heavyweight title, Ali had to beat George Foreman. In 1974, the two boxers agreed to fight, not in the United States but in the African nation of Zaire (now called the Democratic Republic of Congo). Each fighter would be paid $5 million—a sum guaranteed by the president of Zaire and other sponsors.

Both men arrived a few weeks early to become adjusted to the tropical climate in Zaire. After Foreman got hurt during practice, the fight was delayed for a few weeks. The fight was set for October 29 at 4:00 a.m., so that people in North America could watch it on TV during regular viewing hours. Like Ali, Foreman was an Olympic gold medalist, winning his fame in the 1968 Olympic Games in Mexico City.

Ali's New Strategy

Every time other boxers thought they had Ali's style figured out, he would change his strategy and come up with something new. In one of

Joe Frazier (left) and Muhammad Ali playfully strike a combative pose together at an event in 2002, long after the bluster and hype of their fighting days had receded into the past.

the biggest upsets in boxing history, Ali won back his title by defeating Foreman in a bout in which he displayed his new tactics.

Ali relied on his ability to take a punch instead, because he wasn't as lightning fast on his feet as he used to be. Instead of shuffling out of the way, he leaned back against the ropes and let Foreman punch at his body so that the other fighter would wear himself out. He called this tactic "rope a dope." Then, later in the bout, Ali moved in and began punching back, leading with a simple right-hand punch. Foreman knew about Ali's famous jabs and other moves, but that was a punch he wasn't expecting.

In the eighth round, Ali delivered a punch that knocked the fearsome Foreman down. That was the end of the fight. He had beaten the odds once more. At 32 years old, 7 years after his last championship, Ali had recaptured the crown!

Thrilla in Manila— Ali vs Frazier, Philippines, 1975

If their first match-up was the fight of the century, then the third fight between Ali and Frazier, on October 1, 1975, could be considered the match of the millennium. Ali and Frazier had each won a fight against the other, and this fight would decide it all.

Both men were battling for their pride, which would help make this one of the most memorable fights ever. Over the course of the fight, both men suffered severe punishment at the hands of the other, but neither of them wanted to quit. Finally, after the 14th round, with Frazier's eyes so swollen he could barely see, his manager stopped the fight. Ali was the winner and still the champion, but the fight hurt him badly.

During his stay in the Philippines, Ali continued a relationship he had begun with a young actress named Veronica Porche. By 1977, Ali's marriage to Khalilah (Brenda) had ended. In the same year, Veronica became Ali's third wife, and the two had two children named Hana and Laila.

Ali vs Spinks, February 1978

In 1976–1977, following his win over Frazier, Ali fought six fights, including a third match with Ken Norton, all of which he won. Ali had thought about retiring, but he loved the feeling of being on top in the boxing world again. Then along came a young challenger, Leon Spinks, whom Ali nicknamed Dracula because of his missing teeth. When they fought, Ali was 36. He was past his prime as a boxer but with a lifetime of skill behind him. Spinks was 24, fresh from his gold medal-winning performance at the 1976 Olympics in Montreal, and he was just beginning his career. When they met in Las Vegas, Ali used the same "rope a dope" tactic he had on Foreman, but the young boxer had too much stamina. Spinks won a split decision. He had taken the title away from Ali.

Muhammad Ali was a huge fan favorite in Zaire (present-day Democratic Republic of Congo). The 1974 Rumble in the Jungle was as historic politically and culturally as it was a tremendously successful boxing match. Here, Ali is shown having fun with a crowd in Kinshasa, the capital of Zaire.

Sparring with Spinks, September 1978

Ali reacted the way he had always done when facing a challenge. He simply tried harder. Ali immediately demanded a rematch after losing to Spinks, vowing to be in better shape. When they met in New Orleans seven months after their first fight, Ali dominated. Spinks had been enjoying his new status too much to concentrate on serious training. Ali won the 15-round match and became world champ for a third time—something no other boxer had ever done.

Ali was getting older, however, and he would have to make the decision to retire soon. The question of retiring or fighting on was a difficult one for him, and his indecision would have troubling consequences.

Punch-Drunk

Contact sports such as boxing, rugby, and football can cause head injuries that lead to concussions or permanent brain damage. Boxers who suffer from brain injuries are sometimes said to be punch-drunk. The American Medical Association, followed by doctors in Britain, Canada, and Australia, called for a ban on boxing in 1983. People who support the ban say boxing is the only sport in which opponents deliberately try to hurt each other.

THE CHILDREN OF MUHAMMAD ALI

Ali has been married four times and has had other relationships that produced children. His nine children are Maryum, Jamillah, Rasheda, Muhammad Jr., Laila, Hana, Miya, Khaliah, and Asaad. All of them have developed interesting, productive lives within and beyond the shadow of their famous father. Here are a few examples.

Maryum Ali has had a career writing lyrics to rap music, as well as acting, performing comedy, and pursuing other kinds of writing. She has also been a social worker, specializing in working with at-risk children in the inner city, and she helps organize events and campaigns to promote research into Parkinson's disease and patient care.

Laila Ali was an undefeated boxer and a celebrity in her own right, who defeated Joe Frazier's daughter Jackie Frazier-Lyde in 2001. Hana Yasmeen Ali collaborated with her father on a book on his philosophy and experiences. Ali's adopted son Asaad Ali is a talented baseball catcher who played college ball and may be headed for a professional career.

Ali has long had a fondness for all children, sometimes showing off his magic tricks to adoring young fans all over the world. His own children also have fond thoughts of his affection for them. Said Hana, "With all of the prizes, trophies, awards, and treasures that my father has received and given away, his greatness lay in the way he kept recordings of his children's voices protected in a small safe."

Maryum "Maymay" Ali, a writer, rap lyricist, social worker, and community organizer, is shown at a photographic exhibit honoring her father in 2007.

Laila Ali, an actress and undefeated boxing champ, does a little mugging for the camera at a Hollywood event in 2003.

Chapter 6
Hanging Up the Gloves

Muhammad Ali's achievements have gone beyond his status as a boxer in so many ways. He was a world champion, but he was also a superb marketing genius and promoter who understood the kind of hype required to capture the public's attention in the television age. He wasn't afraid to stand firm in his beliefs, even when they made him unpopular and threatened to destroy his career. His personality propelled him to a new level of respect in the same way his physical strength did. He then used his fame to bring attention to less fortunate people around the world and work for an end to conflict in some of the planet's war-torn areas.

> *"All of my life, if I wanted to do something I studied those who were good at it; then I memorized what I learned, and believed that I could do it, too. Then I went out and did it."*
>
> Muhammad Ali

Retirement, Again and Again

Before Ali could seal his place as a public figure and begin realizing his legacy as a humanitarian, he had to let go of boxing. For an athlete like Muhammad Ali, it can be difficult to know whether to quit when one is still winning. After spending a career training for the brief and satisfying moment of becoming number one in the field, how easy, or difficult, can it be to stop? Ali occasionally talked about retirement. He was no more eager to face the end of his career in the 1970s, however, than he had been in the 1960s after being kicked out of boxing.

Although Ali knew that his signature speed and lightning-fast reactions were slowing down, he still believed his own hype. Not all his handlers believed the hype, however. His personal physician, Dr. Ferdie Pacheco, quit in 1977 after he was unable to convince Ali that continuing to fight would permanently harm his health. That year, Ali had managed to win against the brutal puncher Earnie Shavers. During the fight, Ali showed signs of weakness that his trainer Angelo Dundee was concerned about. Ali outlasted Shavers, but the bout took its toll on him.

After he had won the title back a record third time in 1978, he was ready to retire from boxing. In 1979, Ali made it official.

Ali's career as a boxer was coming to an end, but his heroic status continued to grow. Fans still called him The Greatest. As his physical abilities declined, his interest in humanitarian and charitable work grew. *Time* magazine called him the most recognizable person in

> *"I'd be the biggest fool in the world to go out a loser after being the first three-time champ. None of the black athletes before me ever got out when they were on top."*
>
> Muhammad Ali

the world. Before moving on and using his celebrity to help others, however, he changed his mind a few times about not stepping into the ring again.

> *"He rode fame like it was a skateboard. He symbolized change, rebellion, and liberation in an era defined by those qualities."*
>
> Author Jack Newfield

It has been said that Muhammad Ali is the most recognized human being on the planet. Dagestan, a region that is part of Russia, issued this postage stamp bearing his likeness in 2001—without identifying him by name!

Ali vs Larry Holmes, Las Vegas, 1980

After two years away from boxing, Ali couldn't resist trying for the heavyweight championship for a fourth time, especially when boxing promoter Don King offered him $8 million. In 1980, the champion was Larry Holmes, Ali's former sparring partner. That meant that after hundreds of hours in the ring with his former boss, Holmes had intimate knowledge of Ali's style and knew all the tricks that Ali could use. In a way, the fight was a no-win situation for Holmes. If he lost, people would say he'd been beaten by an old man. If he won, they'd say he had just beaten an old man.

Holmes had plenty of respect for his former employer. He agreed to go ahead with the match. Ali went ahead, even though some people feared for his health.

The fight was dominated by Holmes, lasting 10 rounds until Ali's trainer Dundee stopped the fight. That was also the bout that put an end to Ali's championship quest for the fourth heavyweight crown.

Drama in Bahama— Ali vs. Berbick, Bahamas, 1981

Despite what looked to everyone like the end of his career, Ali had one more fight in him—on December 11, 1981, against Jamaican-Canadian heavyweight Trevor Berbick. Because none of the U.S. boxing groups would allow them to hold a fight due to concerns about Ali's health, promoters arranged to hold it in the Bahamas. The familiar hype dubbed it the Drama in Bahama, but few people believed the

Larry Holmes holds a trophy naming him one of the Ten Outstanding Americans of 1979, presented by the Jaycees (United States Junior Chamber), an American public-service organization. Holmes, once a sparring partner of Muhammad Ali and several other top fighters, defended his heavyweight crown against his former boss in 1980.

BOXING REFORM

The sport of boxing has historically been tainted by corruption and taking unfair advantage of the fighters, who often ended up with little money, while greedy dishonest promoters made a fortune. The Muhammad Ali Boxing Reform Act, a federal law passed in 2000, aims to regulate the types of contracts that fighters can sign and demands more financial disclosure so the division of the fight revenue is known by all involved. The law also protects the safety of the fighters and ensures that judging and scoring rules are enforced.

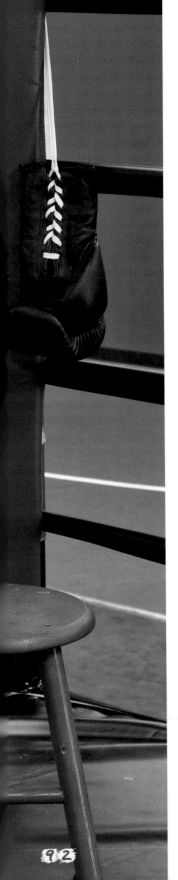

outcome would favor Ali. Yet, he had convinced himself it was the weakening effects of thyroid medication and resulting quick weight loss that had contributed to his battering defeat by Larry Holmes the year before. This fight would be different, he told himself.

A victory for Ali was not to be. Berbick was a fit 27 years old, and Ali was slowing down and nearly 40. In a sluggish fight, Berbick won a unanimous decision after 10 rounds. Ali was just relieved that he hadn't been knocked down in what would prove to be his last fight, the way boxing great Joe Louis had been years earlier. He finished his career with an impressive 56 wins and 5 losses.

> *"I could never really say goodbye to boxing, so boxing said goodbye to me."*
>
> Muhammad Ali

Devastating Diagnosis

In 1984, only about three years after his last fight, Ali was diagnosed with Parkinson's disease—a disabling condition that has left him with reduced movement and affected his ability to speak. The effects of repeated punches over a career in the ring were already evident in his slower speech. The man who earlier could recite his rhymes and chatter to reporters was very quiet now. Although Ali's mind remained sharp, the man who said he could leave the ring still "pretty" because he could dodge the punches could no longer evade the punishment. The beatings he took, especially in his last few fights against Shavers, Holmes, and Berbick, most likely contributed to the head injuries that brought on symptoms of Parkinson's.

In typical Ali style, he made Parkinson's one of his causes, lending his name to the Muhammad Ali Parkinson Center in Phoenix, Arizona, which opened in 1997. His annual Celebrity Fight Night event has raised over $45 million for the center.

Muhammad Ali's surprise appearance as the final torchbearer and lighter of the Olympic flame at the 1996 Atlanta Games was a breathtaking moment.

"In 1960, I shocked the world and won the gold medal in boxing at the Rome Olympics. In 1996, I showed the world that Parkinson's disease hadn't defeated me."

Muhammad Ali, on his appearance at the 1996 Atlanta Olympics

Through his post-ring activities and many public appearances, Ali has also demonstrated what people living with Parkinson's can do in spite of the condition. The world cheered him on as he lit the Olympic flame in a memorable appearance as the final torchbearer at the 1996 Atlanta Olympics. In 2012, billions around the world watched his heartwarming appearance at the 2012 London Olympics. Although he was in a wheelchair, he stood long enough to be a symbolic flag-bearer with other world figures.

Parkinson's Disease

Parkinson's disease is a condition of the nervous system that causes cells to stop producing dopamine, which is a chemical that delivers messages to the brain. As a result, a person's muscles cannot be properly controlled, causing tremors and problems with walking and speaking. The cause of Parkinson's is unknown, but boxers and other athletes who suffer frequent hits to the head often suffer from similar symptoms later in life.

A Place in History

By winning the heavyweight championship three times, something no one had ever done before, Ali earned a place in history. As a result, he was named Fighter of the Year by *Ring* magazine more times than any other boxer, and he was inducted into the International Boxing Hall of Fame in 1990. He won countless other awards, honors, and accolades as well. Boxing experts have had time to consider how Ali ranks against other famous champions, and he is mentioned by many historians as one of the top boxers in history. *Ring* magazine ranked him the number one heavyweight of all time, as did the Associated Press. ESPN, the sports cable network, ranked him second behind Joe Louis, while ESPN.com ranked him second behind his idol Sugar Ray Robinson.

Shift in the 1970s

As Ali's career was ending, society was changing rapidly. The protests of the 1960s led to large-scale social changes in the 1970s. The assumption that one race or culture would dominate others was slowly worn away by the celebration of cultural and racial diversity. The phrase "black is beautiful" instilled pride in African Americans who were finally getting ahead in school and the workplace. This was due in part to affirmative action programs that gave them increased opportunities and opened up the eyes of white employers and co-workers to the value of a more diverse workplace.

Movements for change in the environment, peace, and the status of women were also thriving. In the early to mid-1960s, people like

Ali had stood out as extraordinary, exceptional, or just "different" in their views and their manner of expressing those views. In the 1970s, these folks seemed far less out of step with mainstream American life.

Moderating His Islamic Beliefs

During the 1970s, Ali made some changes to his religious beliefs once again. Although he remained a devout Muslim, he was unhappy with many of the radical ideas of the Nation of

UNDISPUTED CHAMPIONS

When is a champion not a champion? When rival boxing groups don't agree. In the United States, there were two main groups: the New York State Athletic Commission (NYSAC), started in 1920; and the National Boxing Association (NBA), formed in 1921 by the other states. Until the 1960s, these two groups, along with the European Boxing Union (EBU), generally agreed on the process of determining who would be champion.

At different times during the 20th century, these groups merged to create the World Boxing Council (WBC) and the World Boxing Association (WBA). In the 1970s and 1980s, two more groups began: the International Boxing Federation (IBF) and the World Boxing Organization (WBO). Each group hands out championship belts, and all four are recognized by the International Boxing Hall of Fame as official bodies that can sanction, or give official approval to, championship fights. When Muhammad Ali returned to boxing in the 1960s, his quest for the heavyweight crown was complicated by the fact that different fighters had claim to the championship under different organizations. Like other fighters, he had to defeat contenders from different groups.

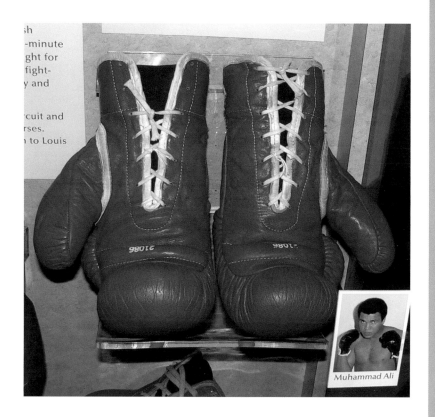

Islam and, after the death of NOI leader Elijah Muhammad in 1975, he switched to the more traditional practice of Sunni Islam, which is the faith that is practiced by most of the world's Muslims. More recently, he has been practicing Sufism, which is a mystical branch of Islam whose followers believe they can become closer to Allah, or God, in this life. They also reject the focus on collecting possessions and wealth as signs of a successful life.

The Greatest Gives Back

Respect, Confidence, Conviction, Dedication, Spirituality, and Giving. Those are the principles Ali tries to live by and the principles behind the operation of the $60 million Muhammad Ali Center, which is a museum

POETIC TRASH TALK

Rhyming bluster was Muhammad Ali's trademark throughout his career as a boxer. He also kept up a stream of creative insults before any fight. "I'm gonna put that ugly bear on the floor and after the fight I'm gonna build myself a pretty home and use him as a bearskin rug," he told the media about Sonny Liston. Liston was not very talkative, but against this chatterbox, he finally read a poem of his own: "O Cassius, Dear Cassius, Go home to your Ma. You ain't got no chance against Liston's paw." Before fighting George Foreman in 1974, Ali wrote this:

"You think the world was shocked when Nixon resigned?
Wait till I whup George Foreman's behind.
Float like a butterfly, sting like a bee.
His hands can't hit what his eyes can't see.
Now you see me, now you don't.
George thinks he will, but I know he won't.
I done wrassled with an alligator.
I done tussled with a whale.
Only last week I murdered a rock,
Injured a stone, hospitalized a brick.
I'm so mean I make medicine sick."

and cultural center located in his hometown of Louisville, Kentucky. The center is teaching these concepts to today's youth through a social media network called Generation Ali.

Ali's early trips to Africa helped him realize that he could use his fame to make a contribution to other people's happiness and well-being. Since then, he has traveled to

Like other boxers who were taunted and teased by the young Muhammad Ali before, during, and after their fights, George Foreman respected Ali outside the ring. During their retirement from boxing, Foreman and Ali became good friends, and Foreman provided support to Ali following Ali's diagnosis with Parkinson's. Here he is shown lending Ali a helping hand at the 1997 Academy Awards. The 1996 film When We Were Kings, which was about the fighters' historic 1974 Rumble in the Jungle bout in Zaire, won the Oscar for best documentary feature and the two were on hand to be among those honored.

countries such as Iraq during the Gulf War (1990–1991) to speak to then-leader Saddam Hussein directly about the release of American hostages, and to Afghanistan and North Korea as a United Nations ambassador of peace. He has met leaders from around the world, such as Tibetan Buddhist leader and human rights activist the Dalai Lama and the heroic South African civil rights activist and former president Nelson Mandela.

Millennium Triumph

At the end of the 20th century, writers looked back and chose Ali as one of the most recognizable sports figures and the most influential sports figure of the century. A 1997 Associated Press study found that 97 percent of all Americans over the age of 12 could identify both Muhammad Ali and baseball legend Babe Ruth. Ali was also said to be the most recognized American athlete in the world. The Associated Press also ranked Ali

"There is no more fitting symbol for the civil rights era than this man who defied all the rules, refusing to be silenced, and did it all with style and grace because of his unrelenting pursuit of peace and racial equality."

Ali's wife Lonnie Ali in an interview with CNN

FIGHT FOR HUMAN DIGNITY

Ali's focus on helping humanity has led him to travel to over 100 countries throughout the world on peace and humanitarian missions. He has worked with UNICEF (United Nations Children's Fund) and the Special Olympics and has made countless visits to hospitals, homeless shelters, and soup kitchens.

In 2005, he received the highest civilian honor, the Presidential Medal of Freedom, and also the Presidential Citizens Medal. In Berlin he received the Otto Hahn Peace Medal for his civil rights and UN work. Amnesty International honored him with its Lifetime Achievement Award. He has an honorary degree from Princeton University.

as the top heavyweight of the 20th century. Magazines such as *Sports Illustrated* named him Sportsman of the Century, and other media such as the British Broadcasting Corporation (BBC) and *GQ* magazine honored him with similar awards.

By standing up for his beliefs and devoting himself to improving the lives of others, Ali added to his sports legacy. He became a role model not only for African Americans, but for millions of people of all races around the world. As a result, his reputation has gone beyond his status as a great athlete. Ali has become an international symbol of achievement and pride for an entire generation of African Americans not just in sports, but in politics and international diplomacy.

Ali has had many movies and documentary films made about him and, in 1999, the BBC named him their Sports Personality of the Century. Even the comic book industry recognized a good story when they saw one. In 1974, DC Comics produced a special *Superman* edition featuring Muhammad Ali.

The Legacy Continues

Despite his declining health, Ali has continued to be active, making frequent appearances to raise money for important charities and events that bring people together. He is assisted by his fourth wife Lonnie, who grew up across the street from him in Louisville and has known him since she was six years old. They were married in 1986 after Ali divorced Veronica. The couple has an adopted son named Asaad.

Ali has encouraged the idea that all cultures contribute to society, and he has honored his own mixed heritage. In 2009, he traveled to Ireland to a special ceremony in his honor

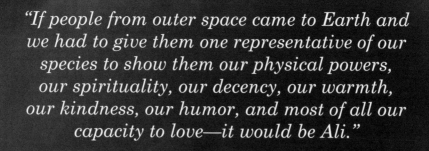

> *"If people from outer space came to Earth and we had to give them one representative of our species to show them our physical powers, our spirituality, our decency, our warmth, our kindness, our humor, and most of all our capacity to love—it would be Ali."*
>
> Comedian, activist, and writer Dick Gregory

planned by the town of Ennis, where his Irish great-grandfather was born before emigrating to the United States in the 1860s.

Even with the challenges of Parkinson's disease, Muhammad Ali has remained in the public eye. There, his name, face, and courageous spirit continue to inspire people of all nationalities, races, religions, and political beliefs in every corner of the planet—a huge achievement for a kid from Louisville who refused to be bullied, believed in himself, and set out to prove he was right!

Chronology

1942 Cassius Marcellus Clay Jr. is born January 17 in Louisville, Kentucky.

1954 Bike stolen; begins training with Joe Martin.

1956 Wins novice Golden Gloves Championship in light heavyweight division.

1959 Wins Golden Gloves Tournament of Champions; wins National AAU light heavyweight title.

1960 Wins gold medal in light heavyweight boxing at Rome Olympics; returns to parades in Louisville and New York; signs with Louisville Sponsoring Group and receives a monthly salary and $10,000 signing bonus.

1960–1963 Begins training and fighting as pro, winning 19 straight bouts, beginning with West Virginia police chief Tunney Hunsaker, and culminating with his first foreign professional fight and a win over Henry Cooper, in London.

1960 Starts training with Angelo Dundee; moves to Miami; meets pro wrestler Gorgeous George Wagner.

1964 Defeats world heavyweight champ Sonny Liston; declares himself a member of the Nation of Islam and changes name first to Cassius X, then to Muhammad Ali; marries Sonji Roi.

1965 Malcolm X assassinated.

1966 Divorces Sonji.

1967 Claim of exemption from military service denied by U.S. Justice Department; refuses military induction; found guilty of refusing military service, launches an appeal of the decision; passport taken away; has world heavyweight title stripped by boxing association and is banned from boxing; marries second wife Belinda Boyd (name later changed to Khalilah Ali).

1968 Daughter Maryum born.

1970 Twin daughters Jamillah and Rasheda born; allowed to fight again in Atlanta, wins against Jerry Quarry.

1971 In the Fight of the Century against champ Joe Frazier in New York, loses after 15 rounds.

1971–1974 Fights and defeats prominent opponents in quest for another chance at the title.

1972 Son Muhammad Jr. born; daughter Miya born.

1973 Jaw broken in loss to Ken Norton; wins Norton rematch.

1974 Wins rematch against Joe Frazier; defeats champ George Foreman in Rumble in the Jungle, held in Zaire (now Democratic Republic of Congo) to win world heavyweight championship; daughter Khaliah born.

1975 In Thrilla in Manila, held in Philippines, defeats former champ Joe Frazier in their third fight (each had won one before).

1976–1977 Defeats Ken Norton at Yankee Stadium; divorces Khalilah (Belinda) and marries Veronica Porsche; daughters Hana (1976) and Laila (1977) born.

1978 Loses world title to Leon Spinks; defeats Spinks in rematch, regaining heavyweight title for unprecedented third time; announces retirement.

1980 Comes out of retirement to fight champ Larry Holmes; loses by technical knockout after 10 rounds.

1981 In Drama in Bahama, loses to Trevor Berbick; announces final retirement.

1984 Announces his diagnosis of Parkinson's disease.

1986 Divorces Veronica, marries Yolanda "Lonnie" Williams.

1990 Helps negotiate release of American hostages in Iraq.

1992 Adopts son Asaad Ali.

1996 Lights Olympic flame in Atlanta for the Summer Games.

1998–1999 Named UN Messenger of Peace; named Sportsman of the Century by *Sports Illustrated*; named BBC Sports Personality of the Century.

2005 Opens Muhammad Ali Center in Louisville; receives Presidential Medal of Freedom.

2007 Receives honorary doctorate from Princeton.

2009 Honored by town of Ennis, Ireland, where his great-grandfather was born.

2012 Celebrates 70th birthday; acts as honorary flag bearer at London Olympics.

Glossary

abolish To formally put an end to something

acquit To find an accused person not guilty of charges

activist A person who believes in a cause, issue, or political system, and acts to promote that belief

amateur Someone who is not paid for participating in a sport or a hobby and may have a lower skill level than a professional who receives money for the same kind of participation

apartheid An official policy of racial segregation that is upheld by legislation (South Africa used to have such a policy)

betting Trying to predict a winner, usually of a sports event, and putting money on that event with the hope that if the bet is correct, one will receive more money back

bout A contest between individuals or teams

convert To change one's faith to a new religion

cornerman A member of a boxer's support team who works in the corner of the ring where the boxer takes breaks between rounds

decision One way to win a boxing match other than by knocking out an opponent; Judges keep a score of who has fought best in each round, and the boxer who has won the most rounds wins the fight

fix To determine the winner of a sporting event ahead of time by manipulating the behavior of players, judges, or referees, often by using money or threats

formidable Inspiring fear or respect through being very large or powerful

heavyweight A weight class for boxers who weigh over 200 pounds (91 kg)

humanitarian A person who believes in acts of human kindness and improves the lives of others

human rights Legal principles of freedom for people (such as the right to vote or to receive equal treatment under the law) that are agreed on by society

integration Combining groups on an equal basis in aspects of daily life, such as at school or work; usually applied to racial groups

Islam The second-largest religion in the world; begun by the Prophet Muhammad about 1,400 years ago

lobby To try to influence others, usually government officials, on certain issues

lottery A process in which the outcome is governed by chance, usually depending on the matching of randomly chosen numbers

moderate Holding less extreme or radical views, as in politics or religion

monologue An address in which the speaker expresses his or her thoughts out loud

odds The relative probability or expectation that an event will occur, expressed as a ratio; For example, seven-to-one odds against a boxer means that his or her opponent is considered to be seven times more likely to win

petty Of lesser consequence or importance, as in "petty theft" as opposed to "grand theft"

polarize To divide into sharply contrasting sets of beliefs or opinions

prophet A person who is in contact with God and passes along God's messages; Moses and Muhammad are examples of two prophets in present-day religions today

race A way to group humans into large groups based on certain identifiable features, such as appearance or bone structure

ratified Formally endorsed or agreed to, as by a vote

reinstate To restore or put something back to the way it was, such as a license to box

round A segment of a boxing match, usually three minutes long

segregation The separation of groups, usually on the basis of race

sharecropper A farmer who gives up part of his or her crop as rent

stance The way in which someone stands

standardize To make something consistent or uniform, such as rules

stereotypical Having to do with an oversimplified view or portrayal in which all members of a group act the same way

subservient Willing to serve and obey others without challenging them

trash talk A form of bragging or exaggerating intended to intimidate opponents, usually in a sporting event

turbulent Violently agitated or stormy, such as a turbulent river or airplane flight

Further Information

Books

Ali, Hana Yasmeen. *More Than a Hero: Muhammad Ali's Life Lessons Presented Through His Daughter's Eyes.* New York: Simon & Schuster, 2000.

Ali, Muhammad, with Hana Yasmeen Ali. *The Soul of a Butterfly: Reflections on Life's Journey*. New York: Simon & Schuster, 2004.

Brunt, Stephen. *Facing Ali: The Opposition Weighs in*. Guilford, CT: Lyons Press, 2002.

Krantz, Les. *Ali in Action: The Man, the Moves, the Mouth*. Guilford, CT: Globe Pequot Press, 2008.

Myers, Walter Dean. *The Greatest: Muhammad Ali.* New York: Scholastic, 2001.

Remnick, David. *King of the World: Muhammad Ali and the Rise of an American Hero*. New York: Random House, 1999.

Videos

Ali (DVD). Sony Pictures Home Entertainment, 2001.

Muhammad Ali: The Whole Story (DVD). Turner Home Entertainment, 1996.

Facing Ali (DVD). Lions Gate, 2009.

Becoming Muhammad Ali (DVD). Tomlinson-DeOnis Productions, 2007.

When We Were Kings (DVD). Universal Studios, 1996.

Websites

www.ali.com
The official site of Muhammad Ali, and the ultimate website for Ali fans, this site has clips from his most famous fights, such as the "Rumble in the Jungle," videos of other people's stories about meeting Ali, a detailed timeline of his career, and a store with t-shirts and posters for sale.

http://sportsillustrated.cnn.com/multimedia/photo_gallery/1006/ boxing.muhammad.ali.tribute/content.1.html
This SI.com photographic gallery offers a remarkable collection of beautiful classic shots of Ali and vintage *Sports Illustrated* covers featuring The Greatest. Separate links lead to more photo galleries, statistics on boxing, and other background information.

http://alicenter.org/site/
This website for the Muhammad Ali Center, a museum and cultural facility opened in 2005 in Ali's hometown of Louisville, features a timeline of Ali's life and career and information on exhibits at the center. There is also an online store for Ali memorabilia and curriculum materials based on principles such as respect, dedication, and giving.

http://ca.sports.yahoo.com/video/player/soly/Y_Sports_ Olympics/30088336#soly/Y_Sports_Olympics/30099088
This website has a gem of a video, about eight minutes long, paying tribute to the life of Muhammad Ali, particularly within the framework of the Olympic Games, as narrated by a number of sportswriters and athletes, including one of his daughters, Laila Ali, who is herself a boxing champion and celebrity. The video includes a synopsis of Ali's career highlights and then a focus on his thrilling appearance and participation in the 1996 Olympic Games in Atlanta, when he lit the flame during the opening ceremonies.

Index

About the Author

Susan Brophy Down lives on Vancouver Island in British Columbia, Canada. As an award-winning newspaper and magazine writer, she has covered a variety of topics such as business, arts and culture, and design.